BEST OF

TALES FROM THE

VOLUME 6

Edited by
Paula Martin Morell and Stephanie Trevino Slagle

Best of Tales from the South: Volume 6

ISBN 978-09846199-6-2

Cover art by V.L. Cox
www.greatfineart.com

More on *Tales from the South* at
www.talesfromthesouth.com

Temenos Publishing
www.temenospublishing.com

For *all* of the Season 6 writers.

Contents

**Winners, Season 6 Top Tales
*Honorable Mentions, Season 6 Top Tales

Introduction
Paula Martin Morell

Season 6 marked a major turning point for *Tales from the South Radio Show.* We changed from a monthly program to a weekly program, added dinner and music to the experience, and joined PRX (Public Radio Exchange), where we won PRX's 2011 Zeitfunk Award for Most Licensed Debut Producer. We also became syndicated by World Radio Network, making the show available to over 130 million listeners worldwide. We added the Tin Roof Project once a month, where well-known Southerners bring their own true stories to life. And, we began publishing a story each month in *AY Magazine,* our official media sponsor. It was a very exciting year!

Because we changed to a weekly program, we featured over one hundred sixty stories in Season 6. So, for the first time, our yearly anthology is the "Best of." As someone who has worked intimately with each and every story in Season 6, it was excruciatingly hard to pick the top fifty-six stories. Along with me and Stephanie, a panel of judges narrowed it down to the stories in this volume, and then another panel chose the top stories of the year for the "Top Tales" contest sponsored by William F. Laman Public Library (winners and honorable mentions are marked in the Table of Contents). Just like in the judging of the stories for this book, we do not differentiate in this volume between the Tin Roofers and the "everyday Southerners."

As with the experience of listening to the show either live at Starving Artist Café or on the radio, stories range from funny to heartbreaking, from life-altering to perception-shifting. One thing they all have in common, as all great narratives do, is the universality that we connect to, so that we can identify with, if not the experience itself, then the emotional impact of the experience, and take away from the sharing that we are better having heard or read it.

I hope that these tales speak to you, inspire you to tell your own stories to your family and friends, and help keep the art of Southern-style storytelling alive. Enjoy!

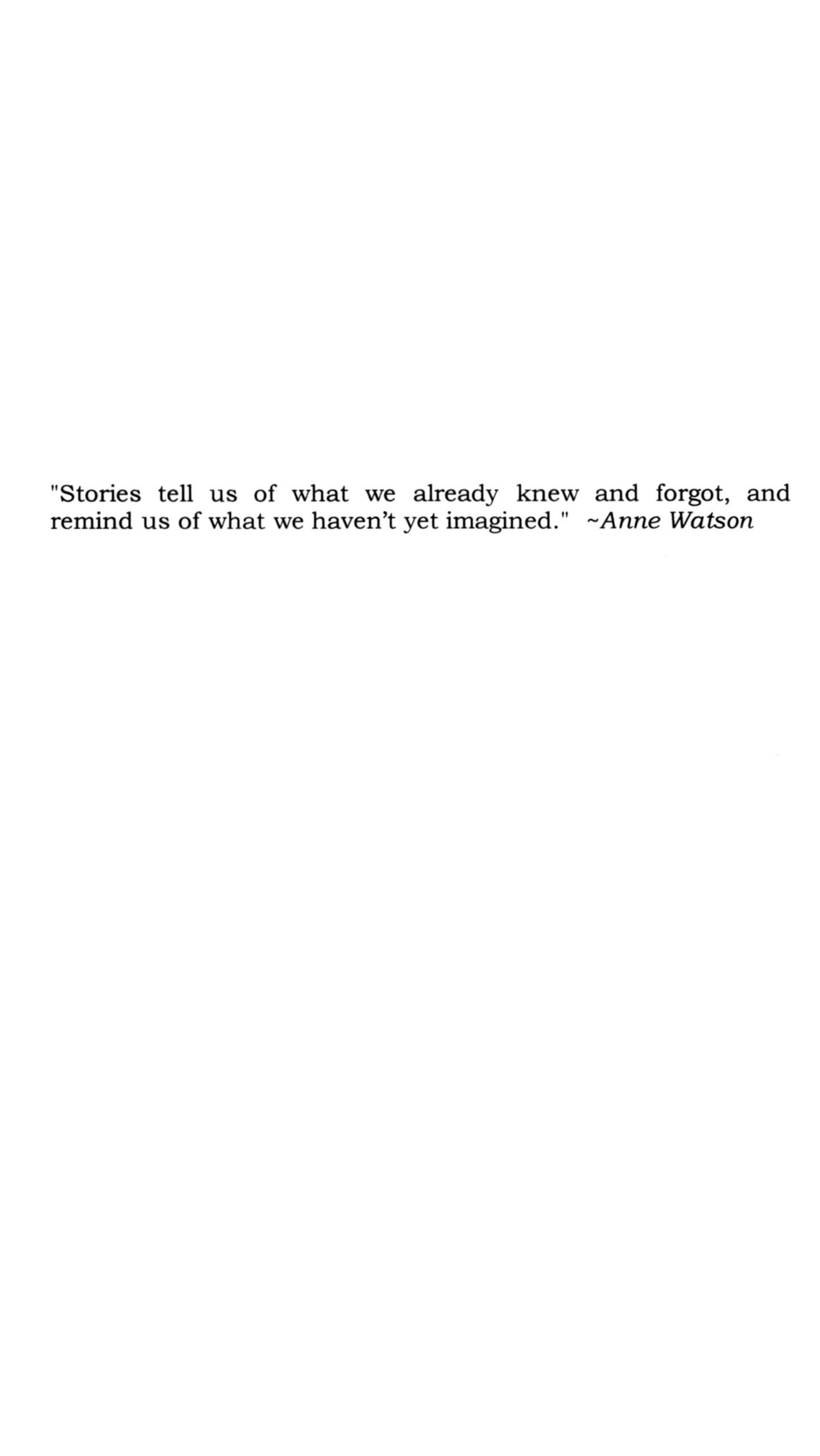

"Stories tell us of what we already knew and forgot, and remind us of what we haven't yet imagined." ~Anne Watson

The Dare

by Grif Stockley

Standing in the doorway behind us, Cootie's daddy, Mr. Tuck Smith, says in that voice of his that sounds like he needs to clear his throat but hasn't in about five years, "Cootie probably doesn't know that after the First World War they killed a bunch of nigras over in Elaine next door in Phillips County."

Cootie and I turn around like we've been caught trying to pee out the back window. It's a close call. Just five minutes earlier Cootie was telling me he's finally found his archery set in the shed behind their house. He had gotten a bow and seven arrows for Christmas three years ago, but Cootie's daddy had taken them away in the spring after Cootie had accidentally nearly shot their nigra maid Maggie while she was hanging up some clothes to dry in the Smith's backyard. Cootie and I are planning later to walk over to McCullough's Hill and see if they still are any good once Mr. Tuck and Ms. Blanche go play bridge later this afternoon.

"I heard something about that once," I lie, knowing I have to say something. I don't know what Mr. Tuck's talking about, but I guess he's just overheard me betting Cootie a quarter that here in Lee County nigras will never be allowed to go to school with us. To hear people talk, you'd think the third world war is about to start over in Little Rock with the President of the United States having the nerve to send American soldiers to Central High School so that nine nigras can go to school with white kids. I say, "The Delta—it's a lot different than Little Rock, isn't it, Mr. Tuck?"

Mr. Tuck draws on his Camel cigarette and lets the smoke

out into Cootie's room. He's squinting at me like he is thinking hard about something, but it may be that the smoke hanging in front of his face is burning his eyes. Just because my grandmother's a historian for the local chapter of the Daughters of the American Revolution and Daughters of the Confederacy, Mr. Tuck probably thinks I know a lot of history even though I'm only thirteen. My grandmother's had some history articles reprinted in our weekly Marianna paper, the *Courier Index* (people call it *The Curious Insect*) under the caption "News of Bygone Days." The truth is I don't care about that stuff and it goes in one ear and out the other. If she told me anything about Elaine, I don't remember it.

Mr. Tuck has trouble breathing, and the smoke doesn't get very far from his face. He starts to say something but begins to cough instead.

"You don't know bull," Cootie says to me, and draws back his hand like he's drawing a bead on me with a bow.

Horrified, I glance at Mr. Tuck, but he is busy wiping his mouth with a handkerchief and studying the contents like he's just coughed up a ruby. If Mr. Tuck is thinking at all straight, he can figure out what's on Cootie's mind. Sometimes, it's not hard. About half the time Cootie acts like he's my age instead of two years older, but I guess that's what makes us best friends.

I like Mr. Tuck a lot, and seeing his haircut stand up so straight makes my hand go to my hair. I push up and back on it, wishing I had brought my brush. Mr. Tuck has the best flattop I've ever seen. Normally, you don't see grown men his age with a flattop, but it looks good on him. I can't imagine my daddy with a flattop, anyway. He's already kind of old at fifty-three. And bald and gray. He comes home from his store and sits in his chair at home and reads *Time* magazine like it's the Bible and Henry Luce is God.

"They got their own schools," Cootie says, and sits back on the bed facing his daddy. "There're as good as ours."

Me and Cootie want nothing more than for him to leave and get out of here so we can get into the shed. But Mr. Tuck sometimes gets suspicious, and we have to act like we haven't got a thing in the world to do. To make up for my ignorance and to try to impress Mr. Tuck, I tell Cootie, "You know our nigras don't care about going to school. It's the Communists behind this stuff. They're trying to tear down our democracy. They showed this film called 'Communism on the Map' in our church about Communist influence and had this map of the United States. Some places on the map they colored pink, but there were some places like Washington, D.C. they colored bright red."

Mr. Tuck nods vigorously, and an ash from his Camel falls to the floor. He doesn't even notice it. "They could take over if we're not careful," he says. "You know there're people in Marianna who'd rather be 'red than dead.'"

"Who?" Cootie demands, his eyes getting big. At least Cootie has put his dadgum hands down. I laugh, pretty sure Mr. Tuck is teasing.

I say more confidently than I feel, "There's nobody in Lee County in their right mind who'd wish that."

Mr. Tuck shrugs as if he knows somebody but can't say. "Are y'all still practicing for an atomic bomb attack by getting down under your desks at school?"

"Every once in a while," Cootie says. "I'd rather practice for a fire drill. We get to go outside."

"Why would they drop a bomb on Marianna?" I scoff. "Seems like it would make more sense to drop one on Little Rock or Memphis. They're a lot bigger and would kill more people. Marianna's only got 4,500 people, and half of them are nigras."

Mr. Tuck grinds his Camel into the bottom of his left boot and drops it into Cootie's trashcan that has tiny major league pennants on it. "I don't want you going in Katie's room," he says to Cootie, "and bothering her while we're gone. You just can't barge in there. If you want something, you knock on her door and wait for her to open it."

Cootie picks up his St. Louis Cardinal baseball cap lying on the bed, knowing he'll get in trouble if he talks back. "Yes, Sir."

I can tell by their tone this isn't the first time today Cootie's been told to stay out of his sister's room. Even though Katie is a year younger than Cootie, she looks and acts a lot older. What she is doing in there I can only imagine. Katie won the "Little Miss Marianna" contest when she was five years old. This year she's co-captain of the junior high cheerleaders. She dates Billy Short who's supposed to start on the basketball team this year even though he's just a sophomore. Katie has at least twenty pictures of herself on the wall behind her bed, and her "Little Miss Marianna" crown is hanging off the bedpost. When nobody else is at home, Cootie and I go into her room and look at her pictures. My mother is always saying to my older sisters, "Pretty is as pretty does."

"Let's go play some catch," I say to Cootie, before he and his daddy start arguing. If he gets mad enough, Mr. Tuck will send me home and make Cootie stay in his room. Being so pretty and popular, Katie gets most of the attention in the Smith family, and everybody else just kind of revolves around her.

On top of McCullough's Hill thirty minutes later, we're already getting bored and we just got here. Even though it's September, it's still too hot to come over here and have any fun. There're way too many thorns and cockleburs and chiggers up here. It's a lot better in the winter when it snows and we can go sledding. Of course it doesn't snow every year and even when it does, sometimes it's just a little dusting. My grandmother says McCullough's Hill is part of Crowley's Ridge that runs from Missouri all the way to Helena just thirty miles to the south. A big earthquake just ripped up the earth a long time ago. I can't hit a thing with Cootie's bow, and he's not much better. We've already lost one arrow in the brush.

I don't know why I say this, but I do: "Cootie, you count to twenty real slow, and I'll take off running down the hill, and you try to shoot me after you get to twenty."

Picking a tick off his arm, Cootie laughs. "Are you serious?"

"Yeah, but if you miss me, you owe me an Orange Slush at the Dairy Queen." Just saying this makes my heart race. "Were you really trying to hit Maggie that day?"

"I was just playing—just trying to scare her." Cootie crushes the tick between his thumb and forefinger and blood spurts out. "It wasn't any different than riding up and down Alabama Street and throwing out some cherry bombs to watch the nigras scatter."

All of a sudden, I begin to run as hard as I can, and I hear Cootie begin to count. He's counting faster than he's supposed to. With all the brush it's harder to run, and he's yelling, "Ten, eleven, twelve . . . "

I trip over some vines but get up and hear him screaming "fifteen, sixteen . . . " I begin to zigzag and put my right hand behind my head as I run. I can barely hear him, but I'm afraid if I look back an arrow will hit me in the face. Suddenly, I hear the arrow zip into the ground to my right. I am sweating so hard I can hardly see. My heart is still going ninety to nothing. I look back and see Cootie running down the hill toward me.

When he gets to me, he laughs. "I thought I had gotten you." I pull my tee shirt up and wipe my face. "You were really trying to hit me." "You said it was okay," he says defiantly. "I was just trying to scare you."

Paean to a One-Owner Antique Car
by Marcia Camp

Time marches on, and that's a good thing. At last, my 1977 Mercury Grand Marquis sports an antique car license. With that plate in place, I can make people think I drive an old car because I want to.

Antique car lovers form not just a cult but a religion. Occasionally while I gas up (which is often), someone respectfully approaches the car and asks if they can look inside. Sure.

Picture this: Saturday morning in Hillcrest, and there's plenty of parking on the street next to Kroger, heavenly king-size spaces that don't require a lot of "backing and filling." I spy a really old car with its hood up; a man is hunkered over, pouring in a quart of oil.

This is not a one-owner car, because the driver is younger than the car. I pull up, park nose to nose, and get out. As I advance, we smile a benediction on each other. We both worship our cars and tithe ten percent of our earnings to keep them running. (My friend Chrissy has irreverently named my Mercury The Pimpmobile.)

I want to ask, "How many miles to the quart?" but that's too personal. I hang over the fender and admire the labyrinth of disintegrating hoses held in place by baling wire and electrical tape.

"Nice," I say. "Yeah," he agrees as he pours another quart of oil into the red plastic funnel. Driving a mammoth vehicle is not easy. Parking is the number one problem—not only getting into a space but getting out. Squeezing a Gulliver-size car into a Lulliputian slot is only the beginning. No matter how I plan my exit, when I return to find my car bracketed by a pair of SUVs, I have to wait for at least one to leave. Even on short errands, I find it prudent to carry a lunch. Forget parking decks.

Then I must deal with disconcerting idiosyncrasies such as an engine that dies for no apparent reason. This would be only an inconvenience except that the power steering and brakes also die, which could turn an inconvenience into a disaster. There is no way to muscle tons of steel where it needs to go, so it's decision time. Shall I take out a brick fence or tangle with a utility pole? I always drive in the right lane and keep my eyes open for safe landing spots. The sign "Soft Shoulders" has taken on a whole new meaning for me.

On the other hand, there are advantages. The turning radius of the Mercury affords a week's worth of upper-body exercise every time I go around a corner.

Now the car has been primped and preened. I've washed the car, lathered the trunk's oxidizing paint with Color Majic, then waxed and polished the deep-dish silver finish to a fare-thee-well. I've buffed the chrome, dressed the vinyl top, and filled the rust holes around the back glass with clear DAP. Just as I get misty about all the beauty, I notice a trickle of antifreeze snaking down the driveway.

Picture this: just off Chenal Parkway, I sparkle down the street (keeping in mind the location of the nearest garage). As I signal to turn into a shopping area, a young man motions for me to pull in before he drives into the street. Is he being a gentleman or issuing a challenge?

I wrestle the steering wheel and thread my way between the curb and the tiny sports car. As I inch by and wave a thank you, I see admiration in the man's eyes. I think he realizes that never again will cars be designed with such conspicuous glamour and dazzling detail. Never again will drivers need so much strength and dexterity, so much raw courage.

Spillside

by Jennifer Pierce-Mathus

Friday night, the second of July, I meet a man I'll call Captain Johnny at a barbeque joint in Ocean Springs, Mississippi. Rushed to wrap up the evening, I am introduced to Johnny by my husband, who offers that Johnny is down from Como, Mississippi, to work the oil spill. I recognize that BP likely contracts him, though this noteworthy detail is somewhat apologetically overlooked in the introduction. Pause. I shake Johnny's hand to thank him for the work he's doing, can only imagine, cleaning up everybody else's mess. Johnny's hands are huge, thick and calloused. His build is farm-strong, looks like a linebacker. Turns out, he is a former University of Alabama football player and a former wrestler as well as a twelve-year veteran of the fire department. He is HAZMAT-certified and trained as an EMT.

I am a native Arkansan, as is my mother, as was her mother. All land-locked at birth. And here in the "territory," even amidst our own natural beauty and if we're really being honest, we live with a bit of envy toward our neighbors with oceanfront property.

Like many Arkansans, that trip to reach the ocean—that long, drive down boring Interstate road, through kudzu and past speed traps and sometimes battleships—is part of my story. That trip to the shoreline represents a frequent, personal and somewhat spiritual mission to find the summers of my youth before the winter takes hold.

Husband is a Mississippi man, brought up mostly in the outdoors and certainly no stranger to the beaches in his own backyard. His mother's Italian family from Clarksdale, Mississippi, makes the pilgrimage each year to the shore out of respect to Papa, who declared his family should enjoy an annual beach vacation and even set aside money in his estate for just that purpose.

So before the well cap is placed, just as tar balls and dispersants and dead creatures begin to reach the shore, but just before family businesses begin to go belly-up and beaches are closed, Husband and I decide to travel down to the Mississippi Gulf Coast to see things before they go from bad to worse, in our estimation. We are compelled to pay our respects. The wake before the funeral.

Captain Johnny heads up a clean-up crew operating out of Pascagoula. All said, Johnny probably is not easily rattled, probably would not suffer fools gladly. On this night, upon hearing my words of thanks, his eyes soften a bit. His breath hitches slightly.

Somewhere, a blowout preventer fails. Weeks of mounting pressure begin to move up and out. He holds onto my hand for a second longer than expected and says, "Thank you. You can't imagine. They've created a Dead Sea."

Husband loves to fish. He and his musical *compadres* head to the public pier to test their lines. Live shrimp bait is running three dollars a dozen. Boom floats in a limp arc around the harbor. Seagulls swoop and dart around in the humid, salty air. A pelican stands watch. Tiny fish flip happily on the surface of the water. Almost as if nothing ominous is happening nearby. And the men fish in the sunshine.

A Mississippi Marine Resource officer casually passes them by, holding signs to post that would effectively prohibit fishing in these waters. Encountering the men, the official—maybe caught up in the idyllic summer scene—announces that for today, he's not gonna post the signs. That the boys can fish.

Had the men stopped to consider the official, they may have found a weariness in his voice. They may have caught his sigh of relief upon seeing a sight so . . . normal.

Moments pass. Maybe an hour. Maybe more. Nibbles, but no prize catch.

Another Marine Resource officer arrives on the scene, issuing game and fish citations to each man. Fishing in closed waters. No fine listed. Court date set. Looking for a fight. Underlying anger under a hot sun. Dead air. No discussion.

The gulls are gone.

Captain Johnny tells his story in leading questions and concrete stream-of-consciousness statements. I can tell he wants to tell more, but time is running out, on our conversation as much as anything.

"Look, my job's safe . . . they can't fire me like they have so many others, short-timers, people who say too much to the wrong people . . . BP is allowing this well to run . . . I'm saying that, look, BP owns the technology, the patent, on the best, most efficient solar panels available in the marketplace . . . I should know, I help distribute them . . . they also have the means to stop this well but won't . . . Salazar rides with me and my crew just about every other week, doesn't say a word. The water is red . . . the amount of carcasses we find every day would shock you . . . I've made it my and my crew's job to try to keep the porpoises away from all of it . . . we work where the water is still green and blue . . . we have a little signal we send the porpoises, and so far, it's worked . . . but, you know, I've carried bodies, babies out of burning buildings, and some days, I'm just not prepared for this . . . I'm telling you, what they have done will result in a Dead Sea . . . one that won't return in five, ten years, or even twenty, or even in our lifetime . . . will I let my kids swim in that water? No way in . . . I wouldn't step foot in it anywhere right now . . . the dispersants can be found as shallow as two feet below the water's surface . . . oh, I brought my kids down here, just to show 'em, 'Look, this is the Gulf, this is what it should be but will be no more.' I'm telling you, BP has destroyed this Gulf for our lifetime."

Captain Johnny offers Husband and me a place on deck the next morning, to go past the red and black and out into the green and blue waters where the Gulf still exists in balance. To see the porpoises and life. Where things still seem . . . normal. Pause. I thank him. I blink hard and tell him I just don't think I can bear witness. I just can't.

Driving past clean-up crews in Gulfport, two men in HAZMAT suits sleep on the sand in the mid-day sun. Shovels or rakes stand upright in the sand, empty plastic bags tied to the handles and catching the wind. Look like strange flags. Flying the oil disaster Standard. But for whom are they claiming this territory?

The judge in Ocean Springs reviews the facts for a second time, after Husband pleads his case through repeated phone calls and FAXed statements. The judge lowers the fishing fines to one hundred dollars per ticket but adds two hundred dollars in court fees. Four hundred dollars even, payable by check to the Great State of Mississippi. Because someone has to pay for the funeral. As we have. As, in so many ways, we will.

Wade in the water,
Wade in the water, children,
Wade in the water,
God's gonna trouble the water.
— (Traditional)

Shame

by Lynn Schaefer

The year was 1973. I was looking out the window of my eighth-grade history class when a tiny, stooped old woman came walking up the sidewalk to the front door of the junior high school. I sat up straight in my desk, shocked. It was my grandmother! She didn't know how to drive, and my mom and her sister had finally talked my grandfather into giving up his car, so I knew instinctively that she had walked from her house on College Street to the school. It was only about a six-block distance, but, for one thing, she was eighty-something years old and not in the best physical or mental condition, to say the least, and, for another, hardly anybody ever walked anywhere in Nashville, Arkansas. What was my grandmother doing, walking to my school? Was she lost? Had she lost IT? Why was she here? Somebody would see her and possibly connect her to me! I would have to talk to her in front of my friends or, even worse, in front of some of the more popular kids by whom I yearned to be accepted. I would have to ask somebody to take her back home, and horror of all horrors, maybe I would have to go with them. I was mortified. Nobody's parents, much less grandparents, came to junior high. She looked like something off *The Waltons* with her baggy old cotton dress and rimless spectacles.

The only child of parents who were forty-three years old when I was born, I was one of the few kids in my group of friends who had grandparents born in the eighteen-hundreds. My classmates made fun of me for the old-fashioned, frugal ways that I had picked up from my grandmother, such as scraping out every last bit of the slimy egg from its shell when we were making brownies. I wouldn't have dreamed of asking one of my friends to go to my grandparents' decrepit house in the middle of town; it had that old-person smell about it, no air conditioning, my grandfather's "razor strop" in the bathroom, and a chamber pot—a chamber pot!—under the bed in the guest room. Most of my friends' grandparents lived out in the country, which was much more prestigious than living in town—there were creeks to swim in, dogs and cats to play with, barns to have slumber parties in, horses to ride. If somebody had gone to my grandparents' house with me, my grandmother might have sat us down to do some embroidery, and my grandfather would have just stared at us, waxen-faced, saying nothing, the way he always did.

Now, here was this grandmother, my mother's mother, at my school. Several minutes passed, during which I suppose she went to the school office and found out which classroom I was in. I was sitting near the teacher's desk at the front of the classroom, which was entered from the back. I heard the classroom door open. I didn't dare turn around to look, but I knew with absolute certainty that she had walked into the room. I heard her sit down in an empty desk in the back row. A few students turned around and giggled. I was the littlest person in the room, but I tried to become even smaller, hiding my body in front of the boy behind me so that she couldn't see me. I prayed for the floor to open and swallow me up. Nashville is a small town where everybody knows everybody else—this very grandmother had been my father's first-grade teacher, and his mother had given my mother piano lessons, many years before my parents grew up and got married—so undoubtedly all the kids in the room, and the teacher, too, knew that the old lady was "Miss Annye Jim" and that she was my grandmother. I wanted to die.

I sat immobilized in my desk, my mind racing—what to do? Where to go? I couldn't call my mother and ask her to come and get my grandmother. My mother was at the hospital in Little Rock with my father, who was recovering from surgery for a cerebral aneurysm. He had collapsed at work at Nashville's only bank a few weeks before and had been rushed to the Howard County Hospital, and then on to Baptist Medical Center in Little Rock for emergency surgery. He had been in the hospital for quite a while, and my mother stayed with an old college friend in Little Rock most of that time, making the two-and-a-half-hour drive back to Nashville occasionally to pick up clothes and check on things at home. I stayed with Aunt Ruth, who was my dad's aunt, and Charlotte, my dad's unmarried sister, who wouldn't allow me to call her "aunt" because she said it made her feel old. I didn't comprehend the severity of this weirdly spelled thing called an aneurysm. When my mother came home, sometimes for just a few hours before heading back to the hospital, I would usually pester her about needing a pep squad uniform or staying overnight at a friend's house or some other matter of grave importance to a thirteen-year-old.

I stood up and marched to the door in the back of the room, averting my face from the side of the room where my grandmother sat. So far, to her credit, she hadn't made a peep, and I guess I thought that if I made eye contact she might say something in her quavery old lady voice ("Lynn? Is that you?") and then my humiliation would be complete and I would never be able to show my face at school again. I would never be popular, never be a cheerleader or on the homecoming court or asked on a date by a football player. I would have to go to school in Dierks, or Lockesburg, or some other town that was close enough to get to every day but far enough away that nobody would know me.

I banged out of the classroom and made a beeline to the school office, my face burning and my heart pounding. "My grandmother is in my classroom!" I blurted out to the receptionist. "What do I do?" The receptionist asked me which classroom she was in, and then she consulted briefly with the principal before leaving the office. I sat down in the office and waited with my face in my hands. I can only guess that the kind and understanding receptionist went to the classroom, led my thankfully docile little grandmother out, and drove her back home. The bell rang; I crept back to the classroom to collect my books, and I went on to my next class. The event was over.

Thirty-seven years later, as I type these words and stare at the computer screen, my face still burns—not from the shame of sharing my school day with my cartoonishly old-lady grandmother but from the knowledge that I cared more about my own reputation than about an old woman who, despite great physical and mental frailty, had remembered which school I attended; had walked what must have been for her a long distance to get to that school; had remembered my name, for goodness sake—she usually went through my mother's, my aunt's, and my female cousins' names before she finally got to mine; all of that to try to get some news about my father's condition, having repeatedly phoned our house without getting an answer. At the very least, I could have walked to the back of the room, sat next to her and held her hand or put an arm around her shoulders, and waited for class to finish so that I could talk to her quietly and then find someone to drive us to her house. Surely missing part or even all of that school day to give my grandmother some peace of mind about her son-in-law would have been worth every snicker, every teasing remark. I remember very clearly how ashamed I felt in that classroom, but for the life of me I can't remember whether any of my classmates made a joke about it.

I also realize that, for the life of me, I can't remember much else about my grandmother, or my grandfather, or Aunt Ruth, and my memories of Charlotte, my father, and my mother become dimmer as each day passes. That, truly, is a shame.

Zeebo, The One-Eyed Coondog
by Kandy Jones

We had only been married a few months, when Ratt came home with Zeebo. Ratt, with two t's, was my new husband, a laid-back Arkansas boy who I'd just married in October. Two weeks later it was deer season, and this Dallas girl wound up at her in-laws' while my new husband shot whatever moved in the deer woods. My daddy loved to hunt, too—why every fall, Daddy would get the gun out of the closet, go to East Texas for a week and come back with white packages of venison. Shoot yeah. I knew about hunting. I'd eaten deer steak. I was Southern, for goodness sake.

Zeebo was a black and tan coonhound. I had a bit of a panic attack because I had heard the stories. Hunters were spending ridiculous amounts of money on these coon dogs. We're talking in the thousands. We were trying to save money to get a little rent house. We were trying to move out of the in-laws' for goodness sake. And it had been a whole two weeks of sheer happiness because I had just found out I was pregnant. So you can imagine my utter surprise when he had come home with a coon dog. To chase in the woods. To wear waist-high rubber boots, a wheat light, and canvas overalls—a fashion "must" when you consider the briars that you can't see when you are chasing a dog through the woods at night to tree a raccoon.

At this point I went off. Severely hormonal and very, very pissed. I do believe I made comments, including but not limited to, the following: "Have you lost your freakin' mind?" "What about the deposit on the house?" "I'm pregnant!" Crying was probably in here somewhere (I'm a crier when I get really mad). "Where in the world are you going to keep him?" "I can't believe you did this." Lots of tears. "Oh my gawd!!! HOW MUCH WAS HE?" I probably also called him various obscene names, but I can't be sure. We were young and I was in love and hormonally imbalanced.

Then came the Ratt zinger: "He was on sale. He only has one eye."

I was speechless. Then, in his laid-back good ole boy way, with an ever-so-slight grin, he added, "Heck, Slick, he was a deal. Only a hundred dollars and he only runs into trees on his right, every now and then."

"Slick" was his term of endearment for me. Not Sweetie, not Honey. SLICK.

We moved into a cute little red brick house in a quiet neighborhood. An old neighborhood where each house sits on about a third of an acre. No sidewalks. Gravel driveways. I loved it. The city girl was living the small town life. And I was having a baby. All was right with the world.

Zeebo had a pen in the back yard. He and Ratt had many happy evenings in the woods. Whatever.

It was spring. Windows open. Folks raising gardens. Money was tight. I was hormonally imbalanced. Ratt got an offer to go back to Dallas and work for a few months at his old job. It was actually a godsend, from a monetary standpoint. We were having a baby. We needed the money. We could handle it. I stayed in our little house in South Arkansas. He came home most weekends. Sometimes I went to Dallas.

Wait a minute. Wait a dadgum minute. What's wrong with this picture? I'm the dadgum Dallas girl. All of a sudden I was ticked off and hormonally imbalanced.

So to get back at Ratt, I came home from a bar (no, I wasn't drinking, just visiting) with a precious little miniature dachshund in my purse. Imagine his surprise when I brought home, what he referred to as a "twerpy" dog, a dog with no purpose. I had my hormonal revenge. I was in the mommy mode, pregnant, new puppy and best of all—I was even. The puppy was adorable. I named her Precious.

Ratt was in Dallas. It was a Saturday morning, around 7:30, and my doorbell rang. Two police officers were there. My heart went into my throat. Precious immediately started barking and would not shut up.

"Precious, pleeeeease hush. Yes, Officers?"

"Ma'am, we're here to serve you with a warrant to appear in court for violation of city ordinance 345-68C-3887-62R."

"Excuse me? I don't know what that means."

"Barking Dog Ordinance, Ma'am."

"Precious, Please shut up!" I plead with my ten-inch little wiener at the foot of the officers.

"Ma'am, seems your neighbors have gotten up a petition against you for obnoxious dog barking in the evening hours." He looks at his feet, and without even a smile, he adds, "Is this the dog in question?"

My pregnant self was about to have a bladder accident, trying to hold back the laughter, "No sir, it's probably the coondog in the back."

Seems Zeebo, the one-eyed coondog, couldn't tell the difference between a squirrel and a coon. Lots of throat. LOUD. Echoes at night. In the spring, when everyone had their windows open. An oak tree with big ole acorns hung over his dog pen. Lots of Squirrels.

BAAAAAAAAAAAAAWWWWWWWOOOOOOOOOWWW!

The situation and the chain of events (a tad boring but necessary to the story, so I'll make 'em short): seems this situation falls in my lap because Ratt's in Dallas. I have never been to court, not even a traffic ticket. I was alone. I knew no one. I was hormonally imbalanced.

I talk to Lawyer, an old friend of Ratt's. He talks to another friend that has a pen and agrees to take Zeebo. Lawyer friend talks to judge. Judge agrees to drop charges as long as dog is off the premises. I have to visit with judge just before court appearance.

The judge called me into his quarters. He was as pleasant as he could be. My heart got out of my throat.

"Oh yes, sir, the dog is gone. I am so sorry. We just didn't know—" yadayada, sucking up the best I could. We talked briefly of Ratt. Small town stuff. Everyone knows each other. He welcomed me to town. Sweet man. He explained that I would need to sit through the court proceedings because several of my neighbors would be present and he had to "go through the motions."

I could do that.

The case was read in court. The judge looked at me and asked if the dog was off the premises.

"Yes, sir," I confidently replied.

Then he slammed the book at me. Banging his hand on the bench, at the top of his furious voice, "And if that dog is EVER seen on YOUR property again, I will levy this fine to the fullest extent allowed by law. DO YOU UNDERSTAND ME?"

All my pregnant, hormonally imbalanced, scared to death, self, could squeak out was, "Yeeessss, sir."

His gavel hit the wooden stand. There was applause.

Two days later, I drove an hour to Texarkana to pick up Ratt. He had taken a cropduster-kinda flight from Dallas. First thing he did? Warn me he had, what he described as, the hangover from Hades. Every ten or fifteen miles, we pulled over. In between the puke breaks, I was steadily reading him the Riot Act. I told him every detail, with expletives. It had to have gone on for at least a half an hour.

He finally asked, "Who was the judge?"

I told him the name.

He took a deep breathe, wiped the sweat from his forehead, got that dadgum, ever-so-slight, grin and zinged me:

"Oh heck, Slick, back in the ole days I slept with his wife."

Miss 1977

by Jack Shock

It was the 2009 homecoming football game between the University of Tennessee and the University of Memphis. We were guests of Amanda, a friend who works at the University of Tennessee, who had scored prime real estate eleventh row center tickets.

We spent a great fall football Saturday poking around in Knoxville where even the trees were sporting Volunteer orange. I had ransacked my closet before the trip. I didn't want to embarrass Amanda by wearing Razorback red. There is a difference between Tennessee orange and Texas orange. Orange is orange, or so I thought. Very regrettably, I chose Texas orange to wear to a Tennessee game.

As we walked up to the stadium, I was immediately awestruck with the floats—yes, floats. We had to wait until halftime to hear the winners. "And the small float award goes to the Pi Phis." The Delta Somethings took large float and they actually said on the PA, "And the winner of the large float category is" while all the Delta Somethings were cheering and carrying on like they had found a cure for cancer. And then it was time for the halftime show.

I was in a marching band for seven years. That's seven years of second chair and John Phillip Sousa and cheerleaders who wouldn't give you the time of day. I know marching bands. I was glued to my seat for a major college halftime show.

First up—the University of Memphis Marching Tigers.

The marching Tigers performed a moving tribute to the recently deceased Michael Jackson, complete with white gloves and a slide around the field to "Beat It" and "Billie Jean." When it came time for "Thriller," each bandie put down his instrument while the announcer piped in the real "Thriller" music over the PA. All those Memphis flutes, slide trombones and flags did the entire Thriller dance, complete with the signature monster mash. When it was over, the otherwise hostile Tennessee crowd rose as one with an intergalactic roar of appreciation to Michael, wherever he was or is. And I was right there with them.

I'm happy to report that the University of Tennessee band favors an old school show. Big hats, lots of trumpets, six steps every five yards. And twirlers.

There was a core corps of about five twirlers, and each could have had a foot squarely planted in five different decades. The frosty hair and all those teeth could have been homecoming 2009 or homecoming 1959. And when you get right down to it, is there really a difference?

And then there was the lead twirler. Her baton seemed to fly just a little bit higher and float just a little bit longer than the wannabees twirling behind her. Her one-piece swimsuit of a uniform was making all the right moves. She handled three batons like an old pro, weaving them in and out in a tapestry that tells a tale of years of practice. I'm not sure, but I think I caught a distinct whiff of her Aqua Net. I was in heaven.

As part of homecoming, the UT band was having a band reunion, and about 200 band alums marched out for the grand finale. As a card-carrying bandie, I have to tell say I was a little jealous. I secretly wanted to be one of those proud old trumpet players out there strutting around in their Dockers and sensible shoes.

But then the trumpets parted, and out came the alumni twirlers. About forty shiny goddesses who were literally just a few feet in front of me and my VIP seat on the eleventh row. The years have been kind. To some. Okay. To most. I find that twirlers generally have good DNA.

I was mesmerized. I couldn't take my eyes off the lipstick and bobby pins. There was even a lead alumnae twirler. Miss 1977. My year. My class. My girl. I alone knew that Miss 1977 was staring straight down the barrel of a fiftieth birthday party. Nevertheless, Miss 1977 stepped just a couple of steps oh so slightly ahead of the rest of the pack, and she took her rightful place as lead. My heart was pounding, and I was drunk on nostalgia.

Some cruel prankster had dressed all the alumni twirlers in nylon tracksuits. All black. No one-piece glittery swimsuits for these old gals. No doubt this was the work of the current twirlers and I thought it was a little rude and maybe even a little bit of an insult. But I myself would not want to be on the fifty-yard line, at fifty, in a one-piece.

The current crop of twirlers stepped aside and stood at parade rest as the old girls busted it out and let me just say those forty batons were screaming with years of pent up energy and sexual frustration. Those wind suit sisters grabbed the spotlight and worked their show, hair and heads held high.

And then it was time for the big finish. Miss 1977 took a step toward the crowd and added two more batons to the mix, throwing and catching all three with the precision of a surgeon. Her message was unmistakable. Baton Cougars rock.

And Miss 1977, with her new nails and bad marriage, rocked her big finish with a triple twirl, caught all three batons and ended with an extended bow that aimed her tracksuit behind right at Miss 2009.

Miss 2009 took one look at all that nylon square footage on Miss 1977 and thought, "no way is my behind ever going to be that big." Miss 1977 gave her the slightest hint of an over the shoulder stinkeye that seemed to say Yes. It. Will. Miss 1977 finally straightened up and settled into her Lead Twirler Pose for one last moment of Saturday night fame, her face glowing warm under the friendly lights of her glory days. And then she faded back with the rest of the cougars to let Miss 2009 lead everybody off the field and back to our real lives.

And right there, in the eleventh row, I made direct and prolonged eye contact with Miss 1977. I mouthed the words I had been longing to say for thirty years: I. Love. You.

And in return, Miss 1977 gave me a wink, a smile, and a reason to live.

The Voice of a Friend
by Helen Austin

Smoke was coming from the dashboard of the car. I'd been hurtling down an exit ramp at seventy miles an hour when I hit a curb and ran up an embankment. This brought me to a sudden stop.

I closed my eyes, assuming I was dead. Then I opened them, saw the smoke, and thought, "Omigod, the car's on fire. I'd better get out of here."

Opening the door, I fumbled for the seatbelt. That's when I heard the man's voice.

"Don't get out of the car, ma'am," he said. As if reading my mind, he added, "The car's not on fire. That smoke is coming from the electrical system."

His voice was pleasant but authoritative.

"Don't move any more than you have to," he went on. "You may be hurt and if you move around, you could hurt yourself worse."

This made sense, but I was so uncomfortable I couldn't keep from squirming. Still, I managed not to turn my head, so I didn't see what the man looked like.

"I've called 911 and an ambulance is on the way," he said reassuringly. "Try not to move until it gets here."

At that point my handbag fell out the open door of the car. He picked it up, read the name on my driver's license, and then handed it back to me.

"What happened, Mrs. Austin?" he asked.

It was the last day of February, 1997. I was driving from Little Rock to Jackson, Mississippi. I got as far as Pine Bluff.

They were working on the interstate highway that would bypass the city and I was headed straight for an unfinished overpass, cruise control set on seventy.

Taking the last exit before the main road disappeared, I tapped on the brake. Nothing happened. I pressed down firmly. Still nothing. I was just yards away from two cars stopped at a red light when, both feet on the brake, I swerved into a turn lane and went through the red light across four traffic lanes and up that embankment.

I related this story to the man. He said something like, "That was quick thinking."

"Well, it sure didn't take as long to happen as it takes to tell about it," I said.

Just then we heard the siren. Help was on the way, but the sound seemed to be coming from several different directions.

"What are they doing," I asked, "circling to land?" I was trying to maintain my sense of humor.

"They probably want to get as close to the car as possible," said the man I now thought of as my friend, "so they won't have to move you very far to the ambulance."

All this time, people had been wandering over wanting to find out what happened. A policeman questioned several of them, including my friend. Then he gave me a ticket for being out of control of my car. By this time I was shaking too hard to write my name, so I just signed it with an X.

The ambulance had finally pulled up and my friend told the driver my story. "Mrs. Austin," he said, "we're going to take you to Jefferson Regional Hospital. Just lie as still as you can while we ease you on to a stretcher."

That was the last I saw of my friend.

At Jefferson Regional they did X-rays and the ER doctor told me I'd broken my back. Then it was another ambulance ride to St. Vincent's in Little Rock, followed by surgery the next day. After about a week at St. Vincent's I was transferred to Baptist Rehab for another ten days.

I got home from the hospital on one of those beautiful, mild, sunshiny days we sometimes get in March. Sitting on the deck of my house, I said aloud, to whomever it might concern, "Life is such a gift." And I thought about my friend.

What would have happened that day if he hadn't showed up? I would almost certainly have tried to wriggle out of the car, which, as he explained, could have made a bad situation worse. The surgeon who pieced my first lumbar vertebra back together told me I'd been within millimeters of being paralyzed. I could so easily have pushed myself over the edge.

A summons to appear in Pine Bluff traffic court came in the mail, with an explanatory note that I could opt just to pay my ticket. The attached police report gave the names and addresses of two witnesses to my crime—being out-of-control of my car.

Wondering if either of the witnesses was my friend, I got phone numbers from directory assistance. But when I talked to them, they both turned out to have just been driving by.

I haven't told this story to very many people. You might say I've held it close to my heart. The first person to hear it was a clergyman who came to see me in the hospital.

He beamed at me. "An angel," he said.

After I got home, I shared it with a girlfriend who brought me some food.

Her face lit up. "An angel," she said.

At the time of my wreck, there was a lot being written about angels appearing to people in difficult situations and helping out, then moving on. But somehow, I didn't want my friend to be stereotyped in that manner. He seemed so, well, human.

Several months later I was sitting around with a group of friends at church. For some reason, I was moved to share the story with them.

"Well there's no doubt," one of the men said, "that God sent someone to help you when you were in trouble."

That was it—finally. An explanation that clicked. On the

day of the accident I was definitely in trouble and God sent someone to help. Not a John Travolta shedding feathers, but someone accessible. Someone real.

The conversation moved on, but for just a moment I was back there in my smoking car on that embankment with the comforting sound of my friend's voice.

Diamond in the Rough

by Bradi Roberts

On a flight from Dallas Love to LAX I found myself seated between two ridiculously attractive people. The Lovely Latina in the window seat was beyond gorgeous: tall and svelte with long legs and tanned skin and shiny black hair. She was dressed to the nines and looked as though she'd stepped out of a fashion spread in *Vogue*. The handsome man in the aisle seat looked like a poor man's Brad Pitt and exuded an air of distinct but approachable professionalism.

It was October 2008, and things weren't exactly stellar in my life. I'd lost my job as a hotel manager earlier that year, and because of my specific geographical location and the global economic crisis, I couldn't find work in—well, any of the multiple professional fields for which I'm qualified.

I'd eventually found work as a dog bather at a pet grooming shop: lifting dogs more than half my weight over my head into a chest-high tub, squeezing their anal glands, dealing with flea dip in my eyes, and facing showers of dirty dog water day in and day out. It didn't help that I'm firmly in the cat corner and secretly terrified of dogs. But I forged on because a job is a job, and those are hard to come by in rural Arkansas.

This trip to Los Angeles was the one bright spot in my life. I was meeting up in person with twenty people I had met online—but first I had to make it through this flight, hopefully unnoticed and obscure.

Just before take-off Lovely Latina realized she didn't need her handbag. "Senor," she said in a deep, throaty voice, "would you please put my bag away?" Fake Pitt gave her a crooked, boyish grin and obliged, putting her belongings in the overhead compartment. Sitting again, he leaned forward and asked Lovely Latina from where she hailed.

"Argentina," she said. "But I live in Houston now. I'm on my way to California to see my boyfriend." She sighed and pursed her perfect lips in a pretty pout. "Long distance relationships are so taxing," she lamented, then broke into a smile. "And where are you from?"

Fake Pitt indicated he was on his way home to Orange County. I thought that was the end of it, but he didn't lean back. "What do you do in Houston?" he inquired of Lovely Latina.

"Well, in Argentina I was a swimsuit model, but I didn't find that very challenging. So now I'm getting a Masters in bio-chemical engineering."

I stifled the urge to roll my eyes, but Lovely Latina said it with such simplicity and sincerity that I suspected she was telling the truth. I tried to shrink into my seat, although it was clear they were not aware of anyone's presence but their own. "And you?" she asked Fake Pitt. "What do you do?"

"I'm a doctor—a plastic surgeon," he replied. And then, with what appeared to be absolute modesty and matter-of-factness, he said, "I'm on my way home from a Doctors Without Borders trip where my team was doing facial reconstructive surgery in Guatemala."

Oh, Good Lord, I thought. Are you kidding me? These must be the two most perfect people on the planet. It was as if I'd stepped into a ridiculous rom-com starring Meg Ryan and Tom Hanks. Suddenly my jersey T-shirt started sticking to me in all the wrong places, and I began to break out into a sweat; I was hotter than a Billy goat in a pepper patch.

It wasn't until I reached up to wipe my brow—my elbow momentarily blocking Fake Pitt's view of Lovely Latina—that the pair seemed to notice I'd been sitting between them the whole time.

I should mention I'm not much to look at. I'm short—really short, having never grown past 4 feet, 11 inches. And despite being thirty-four at the time, thanks to my good genes and my slight stature I looked like I was a decade younger.

"Oh, hello!" Fake Pitt said, his eyes refocusing to take me in now that he'd noticed my appearance. "And where are you from?"

I opened my eyes wide, wondering what had happened to my apparent invisibility cloak. *Oh, sweet baby Jesus*, I thought. Here we go. This is the part where people hear me talk and I belatedly remember I should use my sign language skills so I can stay deadly silent.

"Arkansas," I replied.

Fake Pitt's smile froze. I cringed. Of course my accent came out even more strongly than usual. I was going for Birmingham Belle and got Billy Bob Thornton instead.

The look on Lovely Latina's and Fake Pitt's faces went from friendly to bemused. "And what do you do in, um, Arkansas?" he asked. He bit the name of my home state out as if it were foreign to him. It was as if I'd said I was from Camelot or Atlantis: some mythical place that rose from its hidey-hole at regular intervals as a gateway to the apparently "real world" of beautiful bio-chemical engineering swimsuit models from Argentina and magnificent medical professionals who selflessly served the poor in South America.

There was no way this was going to end well, and I knew it. What was I going to do? Say I was a dog bather? And then hurriedly throw in that I'd been a professional journalist, a teacher, a minister and a hotel manager? Yeah, that would go over well. I glanced around—ostensibly to make sure no one was listening—and then murmured in a low voice, "I'm an international jewel thief."

Fake Pitt crossed his arms and leaned back in his seat for the first time since he'd put Lovely Latina's bag in the overhead compartment. She, meanwhile, looked similarly flabbergasted.

They both took in my slight frame and deceivingly youthful appearance. "Really?" he said with his eyebrow arched. "Because you don't look like an international jewel thief."

I cast around another furtive glance and then leaned in conspiratorially. "That's the point," I whispered, winking at Lovely Latina.

And then I put in my ear buds, settled back in my seat, and opened the copy of *Sky Mall* magazine helpfully provided by the airline—satisfied no one would bother me the rest of the flight.

Nothing Left But the Pictures
by Arthur Paul Bowen

I first got the word a week or so before that Thanksgiving that Uncle Ralph's wife was in the hospital in Searcy. She had just undergone emergency by-pass surgery. A tiny woman, Ginger had been in poor health for some time due to obstructive pulmonary disease and allergies. Nobody in the family seemed to know that she had heart problems as well. That's country folks for you. Don't tell anybody anything other than the bare minimum. Don't want folks to worry. Or worse, feel sorry for you.

She seemed to be doing better after the surgery. But that didn't last long and after a couple of days the word from the hospital was that she had taken a turn for the worst. I got up there early the morning after getting this news. After I entered the hospital, I looked through the glass in the door of the little family room where Uncle Ralph had spent the last two nights. Ralph was alone in the room. He was sitting in a recliner staring at nothing in particular. I let myself in.

"Boy am I glad to see you," he said as he stood up to hug me. "I was afraid I was gonna have to do this by myself."

Uh-oh, I thought. *Do what?*

"What's going on?" I asked.

"I talked to the doctor this morning," he said. "They say her lungs are filling up with fluid. They can drain her off but it won't do no good. They will just keep filling up.

And now her kidneys aren't workin'. They can keep her alive for who knows how long but she ain't never gonna get better."

"What do you want to do?" I asked. It was a rhetorical

question. I knew the answer.

He sat back down in the recliner.

"Ginger and I talked about this last week. She told me that she didn't want to be hooked up to no machine if she wasn't ever going to get better. The doctors told me it ain't no use . . ."

I just let him talk. My Uncle Ralph is not a complicated guy. He once evicted the guy that was renting the old home place with a .357 on Christmas Eve. Given to nuanced planning Ralph Bivens is not.

But this was the biggest decision he was ever going to make in his life and so he needed to work it all out in his head as best he could. The poor man, being exhausted as he was, must have repeated the substance of their conversation at least three times over the ensuing forty-five minutes. Each time the story began with "Ginger and I talked about it last week." And each time I acted as if I were hearing it for the first time.

"Let's go tell the nurses," he finally said. We went back through the big double doors to the ICU where Ginger was lying. Her eyes were fixed at a point in the heavens. She was struggling piteously to breathe, her tiny chest heaving up and down. Dear God in Heaven. It was time.

"I want this to end," Ralph told the ICU nurse who was standing by the machine that was keeping Ginger tethered to this shore. "Ginger wouldn't want this."

"I understand," the nurse whispered as she squeezed Ralph's arm. "We have to get permission from the doctor to begin the procedure. And he has to be in the room to order us to turn the machine off. I'll call you once I make the arrangements."

We returned to the relative sanctuary of the family room to await the call. Ralph collapsed into the recliner. He put his head in his hands. I knelt before him.

"You're doing the right thing," I said. "Even if by some miracle she survived, she would be bedfast in a nursing home somewhere on dialysis. Her lungs have to be damaged now worse than they were and God knows if her heart would get better. You're doing the right thing."

He shook his head back and forth in his hands.

"No. God, no. She wouldn't want that. I promised I wouldn't let that happen. I promised her."

After a few minutes the phone on the wall rang. Ralph took the call. It was the nurse. It was time.

Uncle Ralph hung up the phone. He straightened his shoulders and pulled himself erect. He smoothed his silver hair back. He inserted a plug of Taylor's Pride tobacco into his jaw. I opened the door to the family room.

"You ready?" I asked. He nodded and together we processed down the long hall to the ICU.

He paused when we got to the big double doors. He turned to me.

"You got any advice?" he asked.

Me?

"Breathe deep through your nose," I said. "Hold it. Exhale. Do it twice." I was training with a boxer back in those days. That's what he always had me do before we sparred. It was the only thing I could thing of.

He did it twice. He nodded. I put my hand on his shoulder and I hit the button with my fist. And we stumbled through the big doors together.

I stayed in the doorway as Ralph said his goodbyes to his wife. The nurse began shutting down the machine. I felt a hand on my shoulder. It belonged to a man who introduced himself as the Chaplain of the hospital. I introduced myself as the nephew from Little Rock.

"Bless her heart," he whispered. "Bless her heart."

"I know. This is pitiful." I whispered back.

"Do they have any children that I need to call?"

"No children. Ralph and Ginger married 'late in life' as they say." The irony of such words coming from my confirmed bachelor mouth eluded me at that particular moment.

"How did they meet?"

"I'm sorry?"

"How did they meet? I'm a pastor. I'm always interested in stories about people."

"You really want to know?"

"Sure. If you don't mind telling me."

"Not at all," I said. "Get this. They first met when Ralph went out there to Ginger's place to do a bush hog job on her pasture."

The Chaplain's face lit up in delight. He dug his hands into his pockets and rocked back and forth on his heels.

"I'll be. What a wonderful story," he said.

"Yeah. It gets better. She invited him back to the house that night for a chili supper. The rest is history."

"I'll be," he said, still unable to suppress the grin on his face despite the sadness of the scene in the room before us.

We stood there in silence for a few minutes. After awhile the Chaplain leaned over to me.

"Guess he did a pretty good bush hog job on that pasture."

"I guess so," I replied, shrugging my shoulders.

After awhile, Ginger struggled no more. Uncle Ralph held her hand as she passed away. The doctor was kind. He assured Ralph that he had done the right thing and that Ginger hadn't suffered. He offered his condolences and turned to leave the room.

"Excuse me, Doctor?" Ralph said.

"Yes sir," the doctor replied.

"Would it be alright if I just sat here a little while longer?" Ralph asked. "Once she leaves this room there won't be nothing left but the pictures."

The doctor looked at me. I nodded.

"Of course you can," he said softly. "Of course you can. You can stay until the nurse tells you when it's time to leave."

And so Uncle Ralph sat there until they brought him the papers to sign allowing the hospital to give the body to the funeral home. And then it was time to leave. My Uncle Ralph had kept his promise.

I will remember Thanksgiving of 2008 and be forever grateful. Because a few days before, with my eyes, I saw steadfast love in action. I bore witness to human bravery. And I was in the presence of the sacred.

Life in the Funnies

by Mara Leveritt

It has come to this: Me, standing stock-still beside my car, at the end of a shady driveway, in front of a house I've never seen before, in Memphis, a city I barely know. And the dog, a huge German shepherd, barking, baring his teeth, straining against a long, taut chain—a chain that, he makes clear, is all that's keeping him off my throat. I stand my ground, reminding myself not to project fear, even as the thought crosses my mind that there probably are times when trying to fake fearlessness is just plain stupid. I am afraid. I am afraid enough that time has slowed down, as it is said to do just before you die, and even with the dog barking and snarling, I can acutely hear every word of the conversation inside my head.

"Now you've done it," some part of me chides. "And who knows you're here? Nobody. Not a soul on earth. That was smart."

To which another part of me rejoins: "But I'm here, aren't I?" "Right. Girl reporter finds her source." "Nobody else found them." "Yeah. Well, let's see you get past that dog."

Actually, the situation does kinda suck. But even with that damn dog, which will NOT shut up, I can see it's also a little funny. White flecks of slobber are beginning to fly out from the sides of the dog's mouth with every shake of his head—as though he already has my head in his jaws. But the chain is holding and, in the tension, the strangeness, the ambiguity of the moment, I admit to myself: this is fun.

The newspaper I read growing up, the *Denver Post*, carried

the comic strip "Brenda Starr." I never thought Brenda Starr made any more of an impression on me than Dick Tracy or Prince Valiant did. I can't remember anything about "Brenda Starr, star reporter," except that she lived in the Lovely Arms Apartments and had a boyfriend who was always off searching for an elusive black orchid to cure his mysterious fatal condition. I certainly don't remember Brenda getting herself into ridiculous situations like this, but the possibility has occurred to me in recent years, what if—Lord help me—I have based my career on a comic strip.

Well, that was a question for another day. Right now, I know I haven't come this far to let some maniacal dog out-bark me. I summon what I hope is an alpha voice and shout at him, "Hey!" He looks at me for a surprised half-second, then backs up and lunges harder against his chain, which I can see is looped around the base of a giant oak tree that stands beside the gravel drive, midway between the house and me.

I survey my chances of circling the dog, calculating the limits of that chain. But I also consider, what if I make it? What if that dog represents fair warning? What if that dog is telling me ferociously: "You do not want to come into this house?"

I still have not moved when, in an instant, the world goes quiet. The dog has quit barking. The front door of the house has opened, and now, standing on the porch, I see an old man holding a shotgun. The dog stiffens and stands at attention. So do I.

My heart races and something familiar kicks in. I know exactly when I first felt it. I was a brand new reporter at a Little Rock paper. It was my first week on the job. The editor came to my desk and said there'd been a fire in south Arkansas during the night. A mobile home burned up. Three children died. Their grandmother lived in a mobile home next door.

"Call her," the editor said. "See what she has to say." "I can't," I told him. "I won't." "Yes, you will," he said, and walked away. And yes, I did call that grandmother.

I told her I was a reporter and that I'd heard what a terrible thing had happened—and that was all I needed to say. She poured out her heart, her story, her loss, as though by telling the newspaper, she was telling the world, and only the world was big enough to absorb the enormity of her grief.

This is that kind of moment. There is a job to do, hard questions to be asked. The man is not aiming the shotgun at me, so I holler politely, "Hello."

"Who are you," he growls.

I take a deep breath. I hate introducing myself at the top of my lungs. "I'm a reporter," I shout. In the silence that follows, I think, "Girl, you know people don't like to hear that."

"Go away," he yells.

"I want to talk to you about Melissa," I shout back. "Not Christopher, Melissa." This is a man whose grandson, Christopher, was murdered, along with two other boys, just a few years earlier. The crime was horrific, sensational. I can imagine he had his fill of media. Then, barely two years later, the man's daughter, Melissa, had died. It was all rather vague. Police said they weren't sure whether she'd been murdered or not. Melissa's death had received almost no attention.

"Melissa," the man repeats. "You want to talk about Melissa?"

"I need to know if the police ever interviewed you?" I shout. "Did Arkansas police ever come here?"

We are all reservoirs. The events closest to our hearts we capture and hold. If, over time, the feelings that attend those events are allowed to drain safely away, the pressure may abate. But if too much, too hard, has been held for too long, the least sign of interest, even from a stranger, can free a flood.

The man turns and says into the house, "She wants to talk about Melissa." He then calls the dog. The animal turns from me as if I didn't exist and meekly trots toward the house.

"He won't hurt you," the man says now, and I believe him.

Then he invites me in and introduces me to his wife.

I enter a room that is tidy, in an old-fashioned, country way. A crocheted afghan covers a chair. I notice a few doilies. But the most striking thing about the living room is the portrait above the sofa. It's a good likeness, only slightly amateurish. I ask who painted it.

"She did," the couple answer together. "She was very talented," says the wife.

We talk for the next three hours, during which I get to see Melissa through their eyes. Yes, they knew she'd had that problem with drugs, but she'd gotten over it. Yes, it wasn't an easy marriage, but that was mostly because of her husband. Yes, she'd said some ugly things right after Christopher's death—she was out of her mind with grief. Once they start talking about Melissa, they are talking about her son too, and about his murder, and about all that accompanied it. I have a hundred questions, and when I feel I can, I ask them. The man and the woman answer every one.

Finally we speak about the afternoon when Melissa died, in a small town in north central Arkansas. I am surprised by how much more I know about Melissa's death than her parents do. Outside, in my car, is a copy of her autopsy report, the one on which the medical examiner concluded absolutely nothing. What, physically, had killed her? He couldn't say. Was her death, at her home, in the middle of the afternoon, from natural causes? Or was it an accident, a suicide or a homicide? He couldn't say that either. I'd found it all very strange, especially since she had not been sick. I also had copies of state police reports on the investigation that followed her death. It was something in those reports that had led me to try to find this couple. The Arkansas State Police investigator noted that Melissa's husband and her older son from an earlier marriage were in the house when Melissa reportedly lost consciousness and her husband called a neighbor, asking him to call 911. The state police had questioned the husband, but there was no mention of the teenage son ever being questioned. I ask the couple if, after Melissa's sudden death, the boy had come to live with them.

Yes, they say, he had. He'd come here almost immediately.

"And have police from Arkansas ever come to question him?" I ask, "To talk to him about that day?"

This—this is the question that has brought me to Memphis. It is what allowed me to stand before the dog and to seek an interview from a man with a shotgun. Melissa died in 1996. I have the state police files, but even today, years later, the local police still will not release records of their investigation. They maintain that, because her death may have been a homicide, they are keeping the investigation open. So I'm stymied. The public is not allowed access to records from an open police investigation. I've come to Memphis on a hunch. Maybe I can find her son, the other person in the house that day. The grandparents tell me he is not at home right now, and it will be up to him to decide whether or not he wants to talk to me. I say, "That's fine." I'll cross that bridge later.

But I imagine they know this much: have any Arkansas authorities ever come here to question him?

The man and the woman shake their heads. "No," they said. "No one ever came."

I look up at Melissa's self-portrait and let their words sink in. I file them, uncomfortably, alongside what the sheriff said, the last time I'd asked to see the file on Melissa's death. "You know, we have to treat it as a possible homicide," he'd said. "We're keeping the investigation open because we're still working it. You never know when a new lead might develop. We've worked it as hard as we know how."

Things were simpler for Brenda Starr. She faced drama, but never real grief. Her dilemmas were all two-dimensional. And episodes came out right in the end. Or, at least, they satisfied.

In my world, a drug addict might also be an artist. A key witness, living just two hours away, might never be questioned by police. In my world, too many truths stay hidden, while hearts break and justice suffers. Living, breathing people struggle to go on with life, covering losses with afghans and doilies, protecting themselves with a dog. I cross the Mississippi River bridge, back into Arkansas, and try to fathom why, police claims to the contrary, Melissa's death was never fully investigated. Why, I wonder, after all these years, are officials still keeping their investigation—such as it was— sealed. I pass through the delta landscape, so seemingly wide open, and I imagine secrets, like ghosts, everywhere. What is it about me, I wonder, that even here, amid these plowed and sun-slathered fields, I fall into such dark and thorny reflections. I question myself and—I get an answer. I see now. I'm not Brenda Starr. It's crazier than that. I am the lover. I am that guy who won't give up hope that somewhere, out there, amid the tangled, jungle of our lives, there lives an exquisite, rare black orchid. The flower's perfume is truth and I—this character of my own creation—need that perfume to live.

Missing Pages

by Amy Manning Burns

One night a few years ago, I was up late—job stress had been robbing me of sleep. Restless, I wandered in to my closet and noticed a stack of journals tucked behind a pile of old T-shirts on the top shelf. These were the chronicles I'd kept for two years after I'd graduated from high school. With a surprised laugh, I took a journal down and opened it. The spine cracked from years of sitting closed and forgotten.

It happened to be the one I'd kept during the summer I turned eighteen and was dating a sweet guy named Cameron.

Whenever I remember Cameron, there is a tenderness that has lingered with me these twenty years. He always smelled like soap and fresh laundry; I loved how that scent would envelope the two of us whenever he hugged me. His hair was milky-yellow, and his eyes were gray blue like old denim.

Everything I knew about men by the time I was eighteen was what I'd gleaned from soap operas, MTV, the occasional romance novel, and my relationship with my father. My worship of one-dimensional celebrities coupled with the emotional estrangement between Dad and I left a lot to my imagination about men.

Although I'd had three boyfriends before I was eighteen, I tended to develop infatuations that were comfortably out of reach. I'd indulge in innocent fantasies about the handsome jock in my typing class or the foreign exchange student with the adorable accent. Then there were the hours upon hours of me holed up in my room and churning out love scenes between a foxier version of myself and a rock star, who, in my world, was always drug-free, monogamous, and the ultimate gentleman.

I was still dreaming about rock stars the summer Cameron and I were together. We spent many a night enjoying the quiet of some random acre of country, lying side by side on the hood of his car on a lakefront, or spending late hours on top of Mount Petit Jean where we had our first date.

Per my journal, our first kiss went exactly like this:

We were sitting on a large, flat rock, gazing at the quadrillion pinpricks of starlight that swirled above our heads in the black sky. First-date tension hovered between us like a third presence. He asked me to tell him when I was ready to leave.

"But," he grinned, "I was really hoping I could swipe a kiss first." Of course.

He slid next to me, pressed his forehead to mine, and kissed me. Cameron had a sweetness he doled out in great lumps, without a second thought as to how it might make him look. If it crossed his mind, it crossed his lips. According to my journal, during another kiss, the wind whipped my long hair around our heads and in between our lips. Cameron looked at me with a sleepy, blissful smile. "I like smoochin'," he said in a dopey way that made me swoon. Another time, I noticed he was staring at me through the windshield of his car. He jumped into the driver's seat and shook his head. "You are beautiful." Just like that. No hesitations. No red-faced mumblings. No self- conscious silences.

Whenever I relived these simple scenes, neurons rocketed around the recesses of my brain. This was a real live soap opera; I was the perfect heroine for this charming, leading man.

My journal entries worsened with embarrassing lovesickness as the summer waned. From the beginning I'd known that my relationship with Cameron would last only two and half months. A French studies student, Cameron had been accepted to a college in France and was to leave that September. My anticipation of this tragic event smacked of daytime drama. I imagined the long goodbye at his doorstep, the tear-filled kisses, and the fervent promises to write.

With each page, an ache began somewhere in the back of my throat. It was a longing for that innocence we all lose as time and heartbreak make cynics of us all.

Waxing wistful, I came across this conversation: "I like you, Amy. I love you." "Don't say that unless you mean it." "Well, I do," he said.

"How do you mean that?"

"Not that I want to get married or something," he shrugged. "All I know is that I do. It's always hard to say it the first time you know."

I re-read the conversation at least a dozen times. Lowering the journal, I felt my brain scramble to search for this memory that I had tossed aside. Then there it was, spinning before my eyes in magnificent Technicolor. I saw Cameron standing outside holding the screen door open for me as I was leaving. His words stopped me just before I stepped out into the hot August night. I stared at him across the threshold, but Cameron, not one for dramatic pauses, turned and led me to my car.

The ache in my throat rose to my eyes, and I began to cry. Why did I forget about that?

I guess I'd always imagined the first time I'd hear those words from a man that they'd be wrought with emotion, uttered on the verge of tears. He'd cup my face between his hands and press his palms into my cheeks with the strength of his sincerity. There weren't supposed to be any shrugs or matter-of-fact declarations made as I was heading out the door. This was the moment that was supposed to blow both of us away and sweep us up in dizzying waves of romantic ridiculousness.

But the moment had come, simply, quietly. It'd been

delivered in the only way Cameron could have done so: with a shrug and with the assumption that I'd known this all along. It wasn't the soap opera scene I'd built up in my mind. Disappointed, I dismissed the conversation then forgot about it.

Our love story had an unremarkable ending. On the day before Cameron left, he rushed around me packing clothes and blasting a Pete Townsend record on his stereo. He didn't cry with me as we said goodbye at the door. When I left his house, I drove my car into a ditch at the bottom of his driveway.

After Cameron left for France, I received several letters and postcards from him. Sometimes he said he missed me. And although I missed him, too, I'd moved on, searching for that perfect moment of new love in the way I'd always imagined it, oblivious to the fact that I'd had it already and had missed it entirely.

I stared at the page that had literally rewritten my personal history in a matter of seconds. Up until that moment, if you'd asked me who was the first man to have ever told me he loved me I would have said without hesitation my first husband. But memory is fickle and selective. It becomes a fixed thing in your head that you don't question. However, a renewed past can yield a powerful clarity you carry into the future. Closing the journal, I smiled at the gift I'd just been given.

Hatching

by Joanna J. Seibert

A young woman with a green shirt is lying on the beach. She puts a stethoscope to the sand. She hears movement. She and two others gently remove a wire mesh previously placed over a Loggerhead sea turtle nest to protect it from coyotes and raccoons.

It is dusk, Orange Beach, Alabama, August 2010. The oilrig that exploded on April 20th and killed eleven workers and violated the gulf with 185 million gallons of oil has finally been capped. Shiny green John Deere tractors pulling covered trailers transporting cleanup workers still patrol up and down the beach. We have talked to locals who report their businesses falling off thirty to sixty percent. The worst hit are the charter fishermen and shrimpers. They have completely lost their livelihood. Yesterday from the window of our favorite restaurant by a marina we watched local fishermen hosing down their boats like boys on a Saturday afternoon washing their cars in expectation for a Saturday night date. For the fishermen the date does not materialize. Members of our family grieve especially for one charter boat captain who frequently took them out to fish. He has committed suicide.

Tonight I sit on the balcony of the condo that has been our family vacation home for twenty-five years. I desperately look out for signs of resurrection. My husband and a half-dozen children gather around the roped-off area where the three people with lime green shirts are removing the mesh in the sand about fifty feet from the condominium. These workers have a shovel, a bucket, a stethoscope and surgical gloves. The "green" team demands that all be perfectly still. Perfectly still.

They gently dig into the sand with their surgical gloves, careful not to rotate and move the remaining eggs in the nest and find six newly hatched baby loggerhead turtles that have just absorbed their yolk sac. Demeter herself could not have been more motherly lifting the two-and-one-half-inch turtles to the bucket and transporting them to the shoreline. The leader in the green shirt makes a trough in the sand to the surf. The sea turtles are placed in the trench and the children cheer as the turtles ceremoniously parade awkwardly to the sea. Loggerhead turtles have been nesting on beaches all over the world for over 150 million years. It takes twenty-five to thirty years for loggerheads to reach sexual maturity. Only one in one thousand to one in ten thousand loggerhead eggs reach adulthood.

I think back to earlier that day, when the bewitching hour of five o'clock approached and nine cars pulled off on the highway shoulder by our condo.

Twenty people dressed in black emerged from the cars and walk to the beach. There is an apparent leader, a photographer. The dress code for beach portraits must have changed from white to black. We watch for almost two hours as the family gathers in various groups for candid shots. The sandbar in front of our condo has washed away and consequently we have lost much beach. The crashing waves have carved out a shelf near the water's edge with a three feet drop off. The photographer uses the shelf for the family to sit on in various groupings. The shelf has made it more difficult to walk to the surf, but how marvelous that the photographer finds a use for it.

Farther down the beach near sunset we saw a trellis covered with flowers. Four bridesmaids in red dresses arrived with the bride and groom barefoot under their white wedding garments. An ancient liturgy has returned to the beach.

It's dark now, and the only light I see is that of my

husband's flashlight as he makes his way back up the beach to the condo. The voices of the children fade as they make their way back down the beach. I can just imagine those baby loggerheads swimming with all their might in the warm Gulf water. Will these six by some miracle be some of the lucky ones?

I hear my husband behind me as he steps out onto the balcony and sits in a deck chair. The rhythm of the waves lulls me and reminds me that the rhythm of life goes on, no matter how many endings, how many new beginnings. I look out into the darkness and say a silent prayer for those baby turtles as they swim into the unknown, as their ancestors did before them.

The Thawings
by Dottie Lou Norwood

With my morning chore of feeding the cats completed, I cozy into my favorite chair by the fire to read one of my new Nancy Drew Mysteries. Mother is in the kitchen putting up breakfast dishes as I hear her asking, "Dottie Lou, was Ginger with the other yard cats when you fed them in the garage?"

"Umm, I don't think I saw her, but she will probably show up later. I left the door open so she can get inside." Before the last words were out of my mouth, Mother was walking into the living room with that look in her eyes that could only mean one thing—for whatever reason, I was in trouble.

"Dottie Lou, you know Ginger is expecting kittens. I cannot believe you did not make certain she was with the other cats. Get out of that chair, put on your hat, coat and gloves; we are going to look for her NOW." When my mother speaks, I listen. She is a strict disciplinarian and has set perimeters she believes her children should obey, and one of those is never to be disrespectful of her authority. Almost before Mother could find her coat, I was standing ready at the backdoor praying for the angels to help us find Ginger so I would not get "the whippin' of my life-time."

During the night an ice storm had blanketed the Ozarks, and the pines are so heavily laden with ice they are snapping and falling to the ground. As I follow Mother down the slippery trail to the barn, I am feeling that big wad of guilt that grows inside your stomach when you know you've done something mighty wrong. "Oh please God, let Ginger be OK."

Sliding the barn door open is really difficult because it is coated with a thin sheet of ice, but we inch it open enough to slide sideways into the dark barn. Mother lights the kerosene lantern hooked over one of the beams, which causes the White Leg Horn Hens to start cackling from their wooden nests nailed to the side of the barn. The pungent smell of the hay along with the soft mooing of Jude the Jersey Milk Cow makes me hopeful that perhaps we will find Ginger hidden in that oh so very cold barn. It is so dark in the barn not only because of the gray day, but Dad had shut both doors and windows attempting to keep out the cold wind.

Mother begins calling, "Ginger, Here kitty, kitty."

I am on Mother's heels as we walk through the dark barn and then we hear, "Meow, meow." Mother walks into an empty stall and there scrunched up under a mound of hay is Ginger and her babies. Mother hands me the lantern as she kneels and begins shushing Ginger as she is trying to see the babies.

"Dottie Lou, take the lantern and go to the feed bin and bring me a bucket."

When I return, Mother takes the lantern, shining it on Ginger and her babies, and it is then I see that tears are streaming down my mother's face. I am shocked and scared because my mother never cries. "Dottie Lou, Ginger has five baby kittens and they are frozen stiff. We are going to do what we can to save her babies."

I stand speechless as I watch Mother fill the bucket with hay and carefully place the five kittens deep inside. "Dottie Lou, pick up Ginger and follow me."

"Mother, what are we going to do?"

No answer except, "Hurry and do what I told you to do."

We troop back through the icy grass, Mother carrying the bucket of frozen kittens and me attempting to control Ginger from jumping out of my arms. Entering the garage, Mother says to put Ginger in the wire cage and bring her some warm milk. I do as Mother says without any questioning.

Walking into the kitchen, I see Mother has sat the bucket of kittens on top of the cabinet and is looking underneath where she keeps her pans. Bringing out a long pan, which she uses to bake biscuits, she then folds several flour sack dishtowels into the pan and proceeds to place the five frozen kittens inside the pan, lining them up as if she were going to bake them. Then she covers them with another soft towel leaving only their tiny heads sticking out. Then to my horror, I watch as she places the pan of kittens onto the top rack of the oven, turning on the gas oven to its lowest temperature setting. Leaving the oven door open, she stands guard, watching as if baking cookies.

Sick to my stomach over the whole ordeal, I lie my head on the table praying for the kittens as well as Mother who I know has gone completely WACKO. Of course, I dare not say one word. I knew even when I was a tiny baby that my brain was wired differently from this woman named Jessie Kay, who was my mother. She has continuously been a challenge for such a free spirit as I am. Many times Mother has said when the stork delivered me, he must have been in a hurry for he had left the wrong baby at the wrong house. I should have been delivered two blocks over to Mrs. Hall. Mrs. Hall is a prissy woman and compliments roll off her tongue like marbles from a jar. Mother is just the opposite; she is a no-frill woman and she never gushes over anything.

So I just sit, and think, and wait for the kittens to bake. But I can feel myself stewing in anger juices and I am trying to wipe this terrible day from my mind. I am also wondering if I will ever forgive my mother for this terrible action. Just as I am about to work myself up into a walled-eyed fit, I hear, "Mew, mew, mew."

And looking up, I see Mother has taken the baby kittens from the oven and is tenderly caressing each one, making certain all have returned to the land of the living. I feel chills running up and down my neck as I watch those five baby kittens with eyes shut tight stretching up their necks looking for their mother's teats.

Turning her attention to me, Mother says, "Dottie Lou, go look in the hall closet, get a cardboard box and snuggle a feather pillow inside."

Bringing it back, I watch as Mother carefully wraps each tiny kitten into a soft cloth and places them into the deep box.

"Dottie Lou, bring Ginger to her babies."

No sooner have I gotten into the kitchen with Ginger than out of my arms she jumps racing to the box where Mother gently places her next to her sweet babies, and she begins licking and counting every one. Mother picks up the box and I promise I see the eyes of two mothers connecting and sharing an indescribable truth.

Without expressing any elation, Mother carries the box into the living room and places it next to the warmth of the fireplace—much unlike the environment where they had been earlier in the day.

Wiping her hands on her apron, Mother goes into the kitchen, and I hear her opening the refrigerator to begin cooking lunch. Kneeling beside the box of miracle kittens while watching Ginger loving each one, I think how often I have wished my Mother were softer, not so stern, maybe more like Mrs. Hall. Yet today I saw compassion that I had heard about in Sunday School. And perchance today I didn't just read about a miracle—I had seen one.

Walking into the kitchen where Mother is standing in front of the stove cooking lunch for her five children and her husband, I put my arms around her and just hold her for a few minutes. She just continues cooking the pork chops and says, "Dottie Lou, Set the table. Lunch is almost ready."

And so I do. But I know.

I know.

The Other Woman

by Betty McPherson

Spring came, and with it the purchase of new living room furniture. After scouring every store in central Little Rock, I finally found a lovely sleigh-back couch and leather chair.

Ahh, the chair: beautiful, comfortable.

On our way home one evening, my daughter, Heather, spoke up from the back seat, "Did you tell her?"

"Tell me what?" I asked.

Father, in his infinite wisdom, replied, "Nothing."

Immediately, I knew it was bad.

Several years before, my husband had walked through our front door with a small creature tucked in his arms. At the time I sent up a silent prayer that a logical explanation existed other than the obvious.

"Isn't she adorable?" he asked, letting loose what looked like a very large rat.

"Adorable? You've got to be joking." I took a closer look; a small dog, russet in color, with curly hair, big ears and a pair of blazing eyes.

"They kept her in a cage," he cooed, stroking the Boykin Spaniel.

"Kept? Cage?" I repeated in disbelief.

"You wouldn't want her to live like that, would you?" he asked.

I could have either been a soft, compassionate woman or express my true feelings. Desperation laced my voice as he bonded with the female. "Please tell me she's not going to live here," I pleaded. It didn't take long to realize all was lost. Lady was here to stay.

The beautiful hand-embroidered bedspread that once graced our bed was no more, tucked back in a safe haven away from sharp nails and curly, short hair. Like a huntress in the night, Lady would search for the softest, closest spot next to my husband. The minute I relinquished my hold on consciousness, a soft bounce would ripple across our mattress. With a snap of my fingers and shove of my heel I could persuade her to move, then, as my shoulders sank back into the pillow, I realized I was losing this war. Morning found her stretched out on the bed, little russet reminders of her presence everywhere.

Then there was the front door set-up. Lady had a fondness for the neighbor's cat and took advantage of every opportunity to make good an escape. My husband accused me of trying to murder the dog. He insisted my motive was to give her access to the street in order to shorten her stay in this world. Now, if the two, ten-ounce chocolate bunnies she devoured one Easter hadn't done the trick, who was I to think that she'd get scored by a passing vehicle? Fact was, when she darted out she went between my legs and I'd grab the door to steady myself. One spiral break to the left leg and crushed ankle was enough for one lifetime; thirty-three year olds and tricycles don't mix.

Finally, there was the episode with the City Pound. The woman working the front desk had been to boot camp, I was sure of it.

"It's a mistake," I told her pleadingly. "I just went over the edge a little bit when I couldn't get all the coffee grounds out of the carpet. My husband thought he was doing me a favor by bringing the dog to the Pound, but he loves that animal and he will hate me for the rest of his life if his favorite female is locked up."

"No. You can't have her back," she stated sharply. The punctual pounding of a date stamp coming over the phone kept time with my pulse.

It was the same feeling as looking into your review mirror and seeing blue lights; that sinking sensation that flows from the tip of your brain to the bottom of your toes. It's bad.

I sighed deeply into the phone. "I promise I will be the kindest, gentlest mother to our—pet. She'll have run of the house and I'll buy a trashcan with a metal lid. I won't get angry at her; I realize she is small and defenseless." I asked God to forgive me for that lie.

"Well—" The date stamp paused; the Sergeant was melting.

"May I come pick her up? Please?" I begged in a hushed whisper.

"Well, I suppose, but we usually don't release pets back to owners who have dropped them off."

"Thank you, thank you so very much. I'll be right there."

Three hours later the mistress of the house was back in place. I had been dethroned.

So that night, when we pulled into our driveway, I didn't panic as I got out of the car and unlocked the front door. Walking in, I turned to the right and that's when I saw the chair. Falling to my knees, I heard a long, slow moan break the stillness of the room, "Nooo . . . "

My fists clinched as I made my eyes open once more to the carnage in front of me. Thirty-five more payments and my dog, my Lady, had decided to claw the leather, leaving streaks of discoloring marks over the entire cushion.

I heard Heather say, "I told you she'd be mad."

I calmly got up and proceeded to lock myself in the bathroom. I mimicked Janet Leigh's shower scene as I slid down to the floor, feeling as if each claw mark was a stab to the chest. I kept my sobs silent as I told myself over and over, "It's only a chair. It's only a chair. Don't think about the carpet, or the bedspread, or the Pound. Don't think."

Through the door I heard my husband's "bad dog," which frankly sounded more like endearment than punishment. And then my mind flew to the many times when he would wrap his arms around me and coo in that Harrison Ford voice of his. I moved to the edge of the bathtub, my head in my hands, and all I could see behind my eyes was Lady's little nubby tail wagging until she was almost airborne when she sensed his presence.

And that's when it hit me.

If I could just shake my backside like the dog . . . .

The Christmas Tree

by J.H.E. "Excy" Johnston

Feeling it might just about be what we needed, I was drawn to the tin Christmas tree in the little shop in Juarez, Mexico, the day before Christmas Eve, 1969. It stood in the middle of a table full of Christmas ornaments already marked down. It was shiny tin, about two-and-a-half feet tall, with maybe a couple of dozen branches and a perfect conical shape.

There was a candleholder at the tiptop and at the tip of each branch. As I moved in to take a closer look at this little wonder, the shop keeper, in her best Tex-Mex, tells me to be very, very careful, to hold it by its base.

I should have listened.

The day before, I had driven from final exams at Texas Tech to my parents' home in El Paso. Although glad to be headed home, holidays at our house could be a bit "iffy," because my mother was severely bi-polar. Most Christmases were really special, but my heart sank as I drove into the driveway; there were no yard lights and no brightly lit Santa face hanging on the wall, not even so much as a wreath on the door.

I rolled in late, but everyone was up to greet me. Dad, not a hugger, gave me a two-handed hand shake, Mom gave me a good hug and a kiss, and so did Mattie, my younger sister, home from school in Phoenix. Mom wasn't looking so good and quickly and quietly retreated back to her room. Dad told us about Mom's latest battle with depression and stated it might be best to just kind of skip Christmas this year, and then he retired for the night. Mattie and I stayed up to visit for a while. She had been home a couple of days, and she thought Mom was feeling even a bit worse from the guilt of not doing anything for Christmas. But the decision had been made: no decorations, gifts, or Christmas church; we just were to enjoy one another's company.

The next morning Mom was up to fix breakfast. While obviously still depressed, she seemed a little more interested in the idea of Christmas. She kept apologizing for the holiday and that she had not so much as put up a tree.

Mattie and I put our heads together and decided to do at least a little something.

We would keep it simple, just a few small gifts, anyone of which would be appropriate for any one of us. We headed off to Juarez, where we would have gone shopping regardless.

Back then, Juarez was a friendly city full of small wonders and delights. Just after crossing the Paso del Norte bridge there was an ornamental iron works shop. You knew when it was open by the Volkswagen beetle parked out front. The entire shell had been removed from the body and replaced with rose vine ironwork in the exact shape of the original beetle body. I loved that car. Further in town was a market with a public plaza.

As an architecture student I was always impressed at how such a large open space could seem so intimate. The market area was made up of small shops connected to each other, each with its own barrel-vaulted roof. Going there was always a joy.

Mattie and I started hitting the stalls and had picked up two or three things and then headed into the tin shop. There were all kinds of incredible works in tin: mirror frames, sconces, table tops, even light switch plates. And the little tin Christmas tree.

Following the shopkeeper's advice, I picked up the tin tree by its base and held it ever so carefully. The trunk was twisted wire covered in tin. Each branch grew from the trunk and had a spine made of that heavy wire. To that was soldered a strip of tin an inch or so wide. Then the maker took his snips and cut into both sides of each strip, creating hundreds of little very sharp "pine needles." I can only imagine what goes through the craftsman's mind before he created such a thing. At the very least, I was sure he checked to make sure his tetanus shots were current and he had a lot of iodine and Band-Aids.

The shopkeeper secured it in heavy brown wrapping paper, then gave us a few dozen candles, each about a half-inch around and three inches tall. She wishes us *Feliz Navidad* and added, again, in English, "Be very careful."

We headed back north across the Paso del Norte, our meager Christmas in hand.

That evening, Mattie and I set up our little Christmas on the coffee table: four presents under a two-and-a-half foot-tall tin Christmas tree. To avoid scratching the table, we made a skirt from the wrapping paper. Dad, hoping this is a good idea, nodded his approval, but Mom did seem to brighten up.

Next day, Christmas Eve, went along pretty well. Mom and Mattie fixed a nice brunch and we had some good conversations about school and life and such. Still, Mom spent a good part of the day in her room. But I noticed when anyone walked past that tin Christmas tree, they seemed to hesitate and on their face would be a slight grin.

That night, since there would be no going to church, we decided to have our Christmas. We turned out all the lights and gathered around our shiny little tree. Mattie and I started lighting the candles. Even before they were all lit, it was starting to get pretty warm in there. But when all the candles were lit, it was a sight to behold, almost beyond description. It was bright, very bright; it was as bold and magnificent a symbol for Christmas as you could imagine. It was also very warm and not unlike a small forest fire.

The dull roar we began to hear was the air being sucked out of the room. The top candle, within moments, had been fully consumed. Then we looked up. The paint was boiling off the ceiling.

As my sister and I began desperately trying to put out the tree, Dad sprinted off, only half serious, to find the lock box of important documents, just to have it handy in case the house burned to the ground. Mom watched all this in amazement with both a smile on her face and tears in her eyes. Mattie and I managed to blow out all the candles, suffering just a couple of burnt eyebrows. After all the excitement, we all just sat in silence for awhile, then my folks got up and went to bed. The paper skirt proved to be very handy, holding a pool of wax, and we decided to open the other presents after the wax they were covered in had cooled. Mattie and I watched a movie on late night TV.

Christmas morning, Mattie and I were the first ones up, just like when we were kids. We had agreed to give each other a surprise gift, but one we could not spend any money on, and it could not be too serious. I gave her my very old single shot .22 rifle, something ridiculous to a gal who had a concealed weapon permit. But she won in the absolutely pointless category; she gave me one of her French textbooks from high school.

Mom got up shortly afterwards in a good mood. She, and all of us for that matter, would look at the tin Christmas tree standing in a pool of wax, and just laugh. Then later that day we opened the four little gifts that had been entombed in wax.

We were all thankful to that tree. It had given us a real thrill. Gave Dad the chance to make jokes on just what to write for the insurance claim on the damaged ceiling. But mostly, for at least a while, it gave us back our mother.

No Greater Love

by Lawrence Hamilton

It was 1972, and I was a freshman at Henderson State University in Arkadelphia, Arkansas. My older brother had just gotten a new car and he and my younger brother picked me up to take me home for the weekend to Foreman, a town in the Southwestern part of Arkansas with a population of 1001 people. I was so excited to ride in my older brother's shiny new car. The trip went great until we got to the exit at New Boston, Texas, which led directly into Foreman. As we approached the exit we were pulled over by the local police. I was afraid as this was 1972, we are Black, and this was the South.

I am the fifth of seven children. Up until the time I was about six or seven years old we lived in a small, six-room tin roof house. Oh how I loved it when it rained. My parents had one bedroom, my three older brothers shared another, and I shared the last bedroom with my two sisters and my younger brother. There was also a front porch, a back porch, and a kitchen. There was no indoor plumbing. A trip to the outhouse was always exciting. I saw many snakes cross my path and the Sears and J.C Penny catalogues were a good way to wish for toys and clothes. They also served as toilet paper. Water had to be boiled for bathing and washing clothes. But I had a ball. I was so excited the day my dad brought home a beautiful Collie puppy, which I promptly named RINNIE after the famous RIN TIN TIN.

Oh the fun I had playing with RINNIE. One day while playing in the front yard RINNIE ran into the graveled road and was struck by a speeding car that crushed his hindquarters.

My eyes filled with tears as I picked him up and carried him out of the road as I thought he was going to die, but thank God he didn't. With seven kids my parents couldn't afford a veterinarian. I had never heard that word. So my dad built him a sling in hopes that his wounds would heal and his legs would get better. It didn't happen. Although my dad tried every remedy he knew to try and save my RINNIE, the flies bred in his wounds and to end his suffering my dad put him down. I will always remember the look in his eyes as he was about to leave me. I loved him so much and so did my dad.

When I was six or seven years old we moved into a brand new house on the forty acres he and my mom had bought across the street. My dad and my brother Dale had worked fearlessly to finish the interior. But with a new house came new rules. No shoes in the house, you never went into the formal living room or my parents' bedroom, your bed had to be made as soon as your feet hit the floor in the morning, do your homework and make good grades, cleanliness was a must, both personally and when cleaning the dishes. The kitchen wasn't clean until the floor was swept and mopped. One day during my week on kitchen duty my dad came in while I was doing the dishes after a big family dinner. He touched the water and found it had gotten a bit cool and made me wash every dish and pot over. He and my mom made sure we did things right always. Shoes shined, hair combed, and we always had to say "yes sir" and "yes ma'am." It always bothered me somehow that little white boys and girls called got to call my parents and grandparents by the first name. Hmmmmmmm?

But my favorite thing was the fact that we had two indoor bathrooms. No need for J.C Penny's or Sears catalogues unless you wanted them. We had toilet paper! "Plop plop fizz fizz oh what a relief it is."

One day not long after we moved into our new house a huge bus pulled up in front of the house. Of course shoes were shined, hair was neat, clothes perfect. Who were these people who made us wear our Sunday best on a Wednesday? You see my parents had bought the forty acres and built the house with the help of the FHA and the bus was filled with people from Washington and Arkansas who came to view the fruits of their labor. These guests included the Secretary of Agriculture Orville Freeman and then Arkansas Governor Orville Faubus. It would be years before I would understand the significance of that moment. I sat there on the sofa in the den with my brother and sisters and stood politely and shook hands as they passed by. When they had left the Sunday clothes and shoes immediately came off and I went out to play.

Unity Elementary and High School was where I attended school until 1970. The school was just one huge white building where all classes were taught, first grade through twelfth. Looking back now I wonder how we survived but it worked. My dad was the principal and my mom was in charge of the cafeteria. After preparing breakfast for us at home she always left early to get food ready for lunch at school. Oh how I loved the rolled oats confection she made called shortnin' bread. Apple crisp was another favorite. My dad was in charge of everything else from hiring teachers, organizing buses and drivers, food for the cafeteria, running his small office, and yes, discipline. I never wanted to get in trouble at school because the punishment would be double. School was from 8:15 a.m. until 3:15 p.m. I would stay behind with my dad and play under the huge pine trees that lined the campus. We called it "the grove." The older kids used it for strolling and courting while we stayed to play in the playground. One day while playing with my friends from second grade class, a truck appeared filled with pianos. My dad called me over and asked if I would like one. I said yes and ran off to join my friends on the playground. I was amazed to find a beautiful upright piano sitting in the living room. I could finally go inside. I began to play the keys and was able to figure out the tune "Twinkle Twinkle Little Star." I started formal lessons with three wonderful women: Cassie Wright, Leola Hatten, who was a contemporary of Scott Joplin, and Delilah Gulley.

In 1970 schools were integrated and I was a little scared. I didn't know what would happen but found out that it was fine. Dad became assistant superintendant and Mom continued to work in food services. I made new friends, joined the band and glee club, and continued to study the piano. In May 1972 I graduated with honors from Foreman High School and with my piano studies landed a piano scholarship to Henderson State University. Wow! College!

The day finally came to leave and Mom and Dad drove me to Arkadelphia to get oriented and settle in. I was filled with amazement and wondered if I would fit in. I joined the Symphonic and Marching Bands, The Collegiate Choir, Drama, and of courses studied piano. Although sixteen or seventeen credit hours was a regular load, I sometime had twenty-one or more. My parents were concerned but I did fine. Because of this I wasn't allowed to come home many weekends as they wanted me to stay and study. On Friday evenings after everyone was gone I would put a rock to gently open the door to the Fine Arts Building so I could return after dinner to practice the piano and organ. Dad would come through on his way to meetings and visit me. It still makes me smile to think about when he would mail or give me two dollars and tell me not to spend it all in one place. I loved my parents so much. To make extra money I played for the St. Paul AME Church youth choir, which was considered one of the best in the State.

And then came the night we got pulled over.

Apparently my brother's shiny new car had a light out and they wanted to give him a ticket. They approached on both sides with their flashlights and saw an empty beer can my brother had left under the seat days earlier. They told us that there would be a $150 fine for the offense.

We collected that amount from our pockets and I was mortified when they told us that it would be $150 each. I knew and felt that I was never gonna see my parents again. They had worked so hard to make sure we were good people and always do the right thing.

I was on the way home to celebrate being in college and being home and they threw my little brother and me in a filthy jail. I was seventeen and my brother was fifteen. As there were no cell phones back then, my older brother drove the sixteen miles to Foreman to alert my parents. We were so scared.

When my parents arrived and saw that we were locked in a cell with a sleeping drunk man my mom possessed the wrath of a lioness defending her cubs. She demanded that they release us immediately, and putting her finger in the officer's face told them, "As long as you live you will never put any of my children in a filthy jail." She was crying and I grabbed her and started to cry as well. I assured her that we were fine.

In the meantime they had awakened a sleepy old Texas judge and my dad kept asking, "What did they do?" They couldn't afford this fine, but if we were going to be set free he had to pay. We finally left and went home completely devastated.

Years later after my dad passed away my mom asked me to help clean out his closet. There were many interesting things found there: Indian head nickels, a certificate drawn on the Bank of the United States worth one thousand dollars, and a letter to that old sleepy Texas judge imploring him to change his mind and asking for his money to be returned. Again I began to cry as I read the note and realized that there is no greater love.

Ozark Beats

by J.B. Hogan

The girl first saw the young boy coming up the sidewalk past the Fayetteville Ice plant. He didn't see her and her boyfriend until they were all nearing the corner of West and Dickson Streets below the University of Arkansas. The boy's eyes got so big you would have thought they'd pop out of his head. The girl nudged her beau to check the kid out but he wasn't very interested and just grunted.

The boy was maybe twelve or so and looked like Beaver Cleaver with his short brown hair, blue jeans, plaid shirt and tennis shoes. He was kind of cute, although so thin he was bordering on skinny. The girl could tell he was fascinated by them. The boy meant no harm staring; he'd just never seen anybody like them before. He was intrigued, that's all.

"He's like all these squares down here," the girl's boyfriend complained, as the couple turned up Dickson towards the university. "He'll grow up to be just another inbred cracker yelling at us, man."

"Oh, Bernie," the girl said, "Cut it out. They aren't all like that. And they're not crackers here, that's Georgia."

"Humph," Bernie grumbled.

"Remember that oldster country couple when the car broke down?" the girl reminded Bernie. "They were way cool."

The boy was walking along the other side of the street, keeping up with the unusual pair but pretending like he wasn't and like he wasn't watching them for all he was worth. The girl smiled at the boy but he turned his head away really fast. That tickled her.

"Don't encourage him," Bernie said, "these hicks will think we're going to reefer him to death or something."

"Bernie, you're like so neurotic," the girl laughed. "You've got to stop smoking before we go out. It's not like home, nobody notices us there."

"I'm hip," he sighed, "I can walk around the city anywhere and there's no crazy Okie bugging me."

"They're Arkies," she corrected him, "and besides we don't have to stay, we can split for home any time we please."

"Don't start that jive again," Bernie said all frustrated, his hands whipping so wild in the air the little kid across the street stopped in his tracks and watched with his mouth wide open. "It ain't cool. I came down here to be with the people and get some material to write about. I ain't going till then, you dig?"

"I dig," the girl said, thinking what a silly thing it was to leave New York where they had friends and nobody called them names and to come to some out-of-the-way Southern town to study people that they, at least Bernie anyway, couldn't stand for a second. *All this for art,* she thought. *What a load of baloney.*

She smiled over at the little boy again and thought she saw a smile flicker on his face. He might even have been digging her, the little devil. Maybe he was small for his age or something and was kind of getting off on a strange-looking chick. That was okay, too. That didn't bother her.

"Come on," Bernie mumbled in that way of his the girl sometimes called "New York Wimpy." "Let's go get some grub. We gotta work in the library tonight and I wanna write later, cool?"

"Cool," the girl said, sneaking another peek at their small shadow, "let's split."

When the couple turned onto Arkansas Avenue heading for Hog Heaven, a real life greasy spoon with great food up past the north side of campus, they saw the boy for the last time.

He had a funny look in his eyes, like he was unhappy they weren't going his way anymore.

The girl gave him a quick wink and a wave but he acted like he didn't see her. He was a cute kid and she liked the way he was interested in them. It made her think all the people down here weren't the same; that maybe some of them might be something different than a hillbilly someday.

* * *

Boy was I surprised when I saw them right down there on Dickson and West. Jeez, right in the middle of town, or sort of, at least real near the university anyway. I couldn't wait to tell Troy and the other guys. I bet they never seen any of them anywhere. I never noticed them till I was nearly at the corner past the ice plant and then I stood there a second until they turned up Dickson and headed towards the university. I had heard of them or something but I hadn't seen any of them before.

The woman was all dressed in black just like the man except that she didn't have one of those little caps or hats like he was wearing and like you see on French painters in books sometimes. She was really kinda pretty and I would've liked to have checked her out better but I just walked up Dickson like I was heading that way and acted like I wasn't watching or anything. Ever now and then they acted like they saw me looking at them but I quick turned away so I wouldn't be noticed.

The guy she was with was pretty weird. I mean he had that little French painter's hat and was wearing dark sunglasses even though it wasn't that bright outside. He acted kinda huffy towards her and he for sure wasn't interested in me. He had a mustache and his beard was growing out, which is strange for here, and he walked funny, kinda like he was bopping along or something like that. You could tell just looking at him that he wasn't from around here. He must have been from up north or back east, but I couldn't really tell. All I knew was that he wasn't from this area.

But now the girl, she was okay. She was all the stuff he was but she was neat looking, too. Her black sweater made her push out real nice in the front and it looked real good. Her pants were tight, too, and made her bottom stick out a little, though not too much. I looked a couple of times at that. She kept looking at me and she smiled every time and once I kinda smiled back but it was pretty embarrassing and I looked away real fast.

They were real different and I liked that, in a funny sort of way. Even the guy, 'cause I figured it must be something to be that weird in a little town like this. I hadn't seen anybody else be it. I wondered who they were and where they really came from. I knew for a certainty that they were going to the university.

Boy, they were something unusual alright, and that was pretty darn neat. And the girl, kinda being nice looking, was pretty cool. She seemed real calm about everything, just walking along checking everything out and not letting anything bug her. I felt that way when she would smile at me. You could tell she was a nice person. I shouldn't've thought dirty things about her but I couldn't help it. She was real pretty.

Right past the UArk Theatre, they went up Arkansas Avenue and that's when I had to stop following them. The guy just walked on but the girl turned back and looked at me again. She smiled me a real nice smile and waved. I sorta smiled back I guess and then stopped and watched them go up the street until they disappeared.

I felt kinda bad when they were gone and lonely like when you look up in the sky and see a plane going over and you wonder who's on board and where it's going. Kind of a funny sadness though, where you feel good and bad at the same time. It's hard to say, I don't know.

Anyway, that was the way I felt and since I didn't have to go home right away I walked back to the UArk and stood out front for a few minutes looking at the preview pictures. After a little bit I took off down University Street past the cemetery and headed home in a kind of roundabout way.

All the way back I thought about those two people I'd seen. For the longest time I could picture them in my mind real good. They were different, unusual. After awhile, though, I couldn't see them so clear in my mind's eye and their memory kinda faded. But it never left me completely. Now and again I wonder about them; wonder where they went, what happened to them, who they became.

Yeah, I still wonder about them—sometimes.

Teeth and a Drivers License

by Susan Elder

December 10, 1992. Two days before my fortieth birthday, I was in the midst of a perfectly horrible day at work when a fax landed on my desk. I managed to pull my eyes from the computer screen to read it—a page of personal ads in the *Dallas Observer*, a free weekly newspaper. As I looked at the top of the faxed page, I spied the handwritten message.

Just trying to help. Love, Doug and Elizabeth.

A little background: Doug and Elizabeth were the same well-meaning friends that lovingly reminded me just the week before that I was still single and must consider that my standards for dating must be a little steep. And if anybody would know, they would.

At a cocktail party almost a decade earlier, I had declared that I would not go out with any man unless he had "teeth and a drivers license." It just kind of poured out of my mouth, and it surprised me as much as it did anybody else. Everyone roared, and I was suddenly the clever, single girl. "Teeth and a drivers license" became a catch phrase with my crowd, certain to bring laughs to any conversation.

Friends would insist that I tell new acquaintances about my dating life. I tried to play it cool, usually saying something like, "Well, the reason I don't date much is because my standards are very high." Then I would pause until I got the full expectant look from them to blurt out my well-practiced line. "Teeth and a driver's license."

While my captive audience howled or choked, they would wave at others to come over and talk to the clever, single girl. I was quite a hit.

However, it did practically nothing for my dating life.

Shortly before my fortieth birthday, I was reminded by these same well-meaning friends that I was still single, so perhaps I should lower my standards. So, once again, after a few cocktails I came up with the logical step down from "teeth and a driver's license."

"A partial plate and a bus pass."

Everybody roared again, and I had my new tag line for my new decade.

And then came the fax.

From *just trying to help* my eyes raced down to a boldly circled ad written in all caps.

> SWF, ATTRACTIVE, WITTY, LIKES TO HAVE
> FUN. SEEKS SWM WITH TEETH AND DRIVERS
> LICENSE. WILL SETTLE FOR PARTIAL PLATE
> AND BUS PASS.

A 900 number voicemail box for interested parties to call was listed in the ad, and my friends had given me the code to retrieve the messages. The responder paid to leave a message, but I could listen for free. This was cutting edge technology in the early nineties, waaay before the Internet.

When I finally stopped laughing, I could hardly wait to start listening. Would anyone actually call an ad like that? And pay to do it??

The answer is—a great big yes. Over the next three weeks, I got over thirty calls. I taped them all.

The very first messages were from men who obviously must have called every new ad. They were very businesslike and to the point.

"Hi, my name's Rick. I like to water ski. Hope to hear from you."

"Hi, this is Joe. I'm out of town until Friday, but please call then. I'd love to go out."

I'm thinking to myself, *Are you guys serious? You're calling me based on what???*

It quickly got worse.

"Hi. I'm Robert, and I don't have a partial plate, but I do have a steel plate in my head. Hahaha. Just joking. I'm looking for someone to take walks in the rain, to look for seashells, to chase rainbows and fly kites with. Then to take naps with, and dream with, and take long bubble baths with . . . "

Oh, Robert. This is your response to an ad that says "teeth and a drivers license. Will settle for partial plate and bus pass?" Good grief.

Then there were the get-right-to-the-point messages. "I hope you're thirty-two or younger because I definitely want to have kids, preferably three."

What????

And a few angry ones. "You specified nothing about age! What age man are you looking for?" or "I'd like to know about your interests. Why didn't you mention that, and I wouldn't have had to call this 900 number."

I'm thinking, okay, so don't call.

A voice that sounded like Elvis reincarnated informed me that he was six-foot-two, ath-a-let-i-cal built, and a part-time pro rassler." I am not making that up.

Another oh-so-sincere voice intoned, " . . . food-wise, I like seafood and steak and Chinese, and occasionally Italian or Mexican." Come on, big guy. Get yourself a taco. Live it up.

There were a couple of great calls. "This is the funniest thing I've ever read, and I just had to talk to whoever placed this ad."

And, "Gee, if we can get our bus schedules coordinated, maybe we should meet for a cup of coffee."

I considered calling those two guys back. After listening to all the nutburger calls I really felt like talking to somebody who actually got the humor. On the other hand, it wasn't like I was the one desperate to find a husband. I hadn't even placed the ad. But it did seem like a waste to have this adventure fall into my lap and not follow through.

So after much encouragement, I made the calls. The first call was awkward, and neither of us suggested an actual meeting. But it made me realize I had nothing to lose, so I called the second guy.

He was thrilled to hear from me. Wanted to know all about the history of the ad, and seemed to enjoy hearing my story. He was a few years younger and seemed nice enough and so interested in talking to me. I started thinking it couldn't hurt to meet a guy who appreciated my offbeat sensibilities.

All of a sudden there was a lot of clattering and banging around in the background. Then yelling back and forth, partially muffled by a covered phone receiver. Finally, he came back to the conversation and explained that he had custody of his three very young children.

No wonder he was so eager to talk. He needed the diversion. And I realized with tremendous clarity that I did not.

Ten years later, as I approached fifty, Doug and Elizabeth asked the inevitable question. Time to lower your standards again? They had plenty of ideas. A guy with walker, full set of choppers, full-time nurse and book full of great soup recipes included, you get the idea. It was pretty tempting to carry on the joke, and with match.com now and eHarmony, there would have been about eight times more responses. But, really, how many part-time pro rasslers does a girl need?

And you know how Oprah says to put your wishes out there in the universe and they will come to you? Sometimes it really does work. For my fiftieth birthday, I received a shadow box frame with, you guessed it, a partial plate and a bus pass. No guy was included, but I figured it was probably just as well. After all, I had already grown to love being a clever, single girl.

Misunderstanding Seems to Run in Our Family

by Daniel Koehler

I'm in the front seat with Mama and Little Bobby, my kid brother. In the backseat, the Libby twins are fighting again. They're always getting wrapped around the axle about something. Mama says they're jealous one might get more attention than the other, but I think they just enjoy fighting.

Mama is driving us to Little League practice in our '57 emerald green Shovelay station wagon. It's a real sharp car—Daddy special-ordered it direct from Detroit because Mama is real particular about her things. She says nothing reflects back on you like your car does, and being a former Miss North Little Rock, she certainly doesn't want to go around town looking tacky. I'm not bragging, but Mama's gorgeous. Her beauty operator swears she looks like Loretta Young's kid sister.

Even when she takes us to baseball practice, Mama gets all dolled-up in one of her nice cocktail dresses, high heels, a good pocket book, and those Mikimoto pearls Daddy gave her on their wedding day. When I was little, I used to call them her "Mickey Mouse" pearls.

Sometimes, I just mis-hear things. I think I get it from Mama.

Right now, the Libby twins, Jerry and Larry, are playing "Gotcha Last" in the backseat.

This is a fighting game where you punch a kid in the arm and holler "gotcha last." Then the kid waits until you aren't looking and hits you back. "Gotcha last" is a game that can get real old in a hurry if you aren't playing.

Now, Mama won't hesitate to set you straight if she thinks you're out of line, but most of the time, she is just as sweet as she can be. Today, however, I can tell that the scuffling in the backseat is starting to get on Mama's nerves.

At that moment, my little brother hollers "gotcha last" and slugs my arm hard. I'm about ready to thump him a good one back when Mama explodes.

"Caleb. Michael. Kellar. Don't you dare hit your baby brother!"

When Mama three-names you, you know you're busted. I unclench my fist.

I think the Libby twins get the message, too, because they stop "gotcha lasting" each other in the backseat. It gets real quiet in the car. "Too quiet," like they say in the movies.

Well, the silence is too much for me. I say the first thing that pops into my head. "Mama, remember Jill Parkin, our old babysitter?"

"Of course, dear." Mama cuts her eyes over at me. "Just a *darlin'* girl! And a wonderful Miss Venable Lumber. She's going to win the Miss North Little Rock pageant hands down."

From the way she goes on about Jill, I think Mama is relieved to end the silence after her outburst. Her voice sounds happy now, like maybe she's remembering being Miss Venable Lumber herself before winning the big pageant.

"But listen, Mama," I say. "I heard Jill wears false teeth!"

The backseat of the station wagon begins to shake convulsively before the first peal of giggles swell in the air.

"My goodness, Caleb!" Mama says. "Who told you that?" Her brow knits and her Revlon red lips part and make a hole the size of a quarter.

"Larry did, Mama."

Mama eyes Larry Libby in the rear view mirror. "Larry, darlin', is that true?" She shakes her head in astonishment. "I mean— Jill's such a lovely girl with such a nice, uh, figure."

Larry manages to gasp, "Yes, ma'am, that's what I heard." His eyes are watering and a giggle escapes his lips like a silent but deadly you-know-what.

Jerry Libby, however, lacks his twin brother's self-control. He rolls on the floorboard of the station wagon, his feet bicycling the air. Chortles erupt from Jerry like exploding popcorn in the hot-oil cooker at the Park Theater. Pretty soon, Larry joins the laugh fest.

I see Mama's face turn as red as her lipstick. "Stop it, boys! Stop it!" Her enunciation is staccato. "Right. This. Minute."

The brakes of the station wagon shriek like the banshee in *Darby O'Gill and the Little People*. We shudder to a stop on the shoulder of the road near the Elrod Ornamental Iron Works building.

It's quiet. Too quiet. Again.

Finally, Mama makes a face and whirls around in her seat to let Jerry and Larry have it.

Some people have naturally mean faces, but Mama isn't one of them. Of course, people who can look mean as a snake whenever they want—TV rasslers, bill collectors, or even those old nuns at Saint Patrick's who smack your knuckles with a ruler for cutting up in school—they have to act mean to keep their jobs.

Mama, on the other hand, has absolutely no clue how to act mean. She's gotten herself in a staring contest with the Libby twins. I can't tell if she is going to smack them or start crying. That's how ladies get when they're mad. To me, Mama's anger makes her look like Natalie Wood in *West Side Story* when she starts beating Chino on the chest after he tells her that Tony killed Bernardo to—you know—avenge Riff and all.

"Don't you boys know how terrible it is to make fun of the afflicted?" Mama's voice gets louder. "My God, boys! Think of that poor girl's feelings! Bless her heart, she must have been in some kind of horrible accident or suffered a terrible childhood disease."

Jerry and Larry look like they expect to get slapped into next week.

Dead air fills the car like smoke in the dry ice well of a popsicle truck. But nothing happens.

When the Shovelay finally pulls up to the ball field at Vestal Park, we all jump out like a pack of scalded dogs.

Halfway to the field, I turn around and look back. Through the windshield of the Shovelay, I see Mama daubing her eyes with her monogrammed lavender handkerchief with the scalloped edges.

* * *

Larry has me in a headlock behind the backstop at the ball field. "You moron!" he shouts.

He is giving me one hell of a noogie with his knuckles.

I beg God, *Please don't let Larry blab it to the whole team.*

But Larry didn't get the memo from the Almighty. "Damn it, Kellar," he shouts. "What I told you was: Jill Parkin wears falsies, not false teeth."

The team draws around us like somebody pulled a giant, invisible purse string.

"Do you—like—even know what falsies are, Kellar?"

I begin to sweat big drops and feel like a bug on a hot sidewalk in the merciless focus of a magnifying glass. "Like—like—fake eyelashes maybe?"

Waves of laughter pelt me. I try to explain, but each time I open my mouth, a surge of jeers blasts me back like I'm trying to take a drink of water from a fire hose. Jerry is rolling on the ground, doubled up. That seems to be his favorite position for expressing glee.

Larry releases his headlock on me. "Falsies are what Jill puts under her dress to make her chest stick out. Fake boobs, you idiot."

Everyone is laughing at me. The older boys on the team,

with their pimpled faces and peach fuzz moustaches, laugh the hardest at Larry's sexual innuendo.

Jerry walks up to me, sympathy in his eyes. He slugs my arm hard and cries, "Gotcha last."

Fight back, I tell myself, but all I do is pick up my ball cap and stomp away. My face feels on fire. Little Bobby is staring at me, his brow knotted up in confusion.

Now I feel even worse. I'm a fool in my little brother's eyes, too.

Baseball practice is agony. I muff every grounder Coach hits to me, and each time I come to bat, someone screams, "False teeth." The team keeps this up until Coach threatens to make us all run laps if anyone says it again.

On purpose, I strike out quickly, just so I don't have to listen to it anymore.

Finally, Coach shouts, "Bring it home!" Mercifully, practice ends, although my humiliation will last all summer.

* * *

On the way home, Mama seems like her old self again. She buys us all lime slushes at Woody's Drive In and hums along with the pop tunes playing on the Philco.

"Larry," she says. "I'm afraid you're mistaken about Jill Parkin's teeth."

The slush-sucking stops. It's quiet. Too quiet.

Larry swallows hard. "Well, Miss Kellar, uh, I didn't think—" He mealy-mouths around a while until Mama cuts him off.

"I did a little snooping around, boys. I called a lady in my bridge club—Dorothy Renshaw? You see, her husband is Jill's dentist, so Dorothy called him. To make a long story short, he said it's ridiculous what you heard. Jill has absolutely perfect teeth."

Jerry looks like he wants to start giggling again, but Larry shakes him off like he does when pitching.

"Yes ma'am," Larry mumbles.

Mama says, "Frankly, I'm surprised at Jill. I mean—the Pageant is right around the corner and she's running all over town with that boyfriend of hers. I swear, he acts so—so—fresh. And he drives a tow truck!"

"That's why they call him 'Tow Willie,' Mama," Little Bobby says.

She tousles my little brother's hair. "I know, darlin'. Still, as pretty as she is, you'd think Jill would be able to find a nicer boy than him." Mama fluffs her hair and checks herself out in the mirror. "I'll admit he is good-looking—in a cheap sort of way." She sighs and shakes her head. "But, bless his heart, that ducktail and leather jacket make him look so tacky."

Mama only uses the word "tacky" in matters of profoundly questionable taste, the social equivalent of a mortal sin on the immortal soul of decorum.

"Tow Willie stabbed a kid once, Mama," I say.

"Jill told me he stumbled. It was all just an accident, darlin'."

When Mama calls me "darlin'," I know everything will be all right. That's her love word.

All the women at her bridge club have love words—Betty Ciapelli's is "precious;" Marge Dickson's is "pumpkin;" Dorothy Renshaw's is "sweety," and so on. However, when Mama calls anyone "darlin'," she means it as a verbal substitute for a hug.

Larry says, "Tow Willie told me they were just playing *West Side Story*."

"Well, I still don't trust that boy," Mama says. She stares out the window a minute like she's trying to think of an "on-the-other-hand" remark to say something nice about Tow Willie, who we all know is the meanest, most irredeemable hood on Park Hill.

"Just take it from someone who's been there," Mama says. "If Jill expects to become Miss North Little Rock, she better not fall in with bad companions. Rumors spread fast at pageant time.”

I hear Jerry whisper to Larry in the backseat: “Yeah—like how she wears falsies.”

Mama hears it, too.

“False teeth?” She laughs that musical laugh of hers. “I swear, Jerry, where do you kids get these stories?”

I decide misunderstanding things must run in our family.

At the light, Mama looks worried. She fiddles with the open top button of her dress and finally buttons it. The plunging “V” in the middle of her chest disappears.

We drive up Highway 107 to Park Hill and drop off the Libby twins. When we pull into our driveway on Cedar Street, Daddy’s car is already in the garage.

Mama rushes inside to greet him, but I am in no hurry. They’re probably kissing in the kitchen anyway.

I feel a tug at my uniform sleeve.

“Caleb,” Little Bobby says. “What the heck are boobs?”

The End of the World

by C. Allan Butkus

It was a beautiful sunny day, and I was walking home from school. I was eight years old, and the world was scheduled to end. There had been quite a bit of discussion around school about the end of the world. Some said it was going to happen and others said it was all a joke. I wasn't sure, but I thought I'd be wise to be safely nestled at home before it happened.

I walked the same path each day on the way home and part of it was through an alley. It was an alley like most other alleys, rusty garbage cans, scrap-wood fences that needed paint and sometimes, other interesting stuff. As I passed through the center of the alley, I saw something glistening on the ground. I took a couple of steps closer before I realized what it was. Someone had flattened a tin can. But it was the weirdest tin can I had ever seen. It wasn't strange that there was a flattened tin can in the alley, what was strange was that no one was around and the can seemed to be trying to reposition itself. It flashed as it tilted from side to side. I approached it cautiously. The can was definitely tilting back and forth. I hastily scanned the nearby drooping fence for scheming faces. None. I flashed my eyes to the battered garbage cans searching for a clue. Was someone was playing a trick on me? No, I was alone. I examined the crime scene carefully to see if someone had hooked a piece of string or wire to its edge. Nothing. The wind wasn't blowing, but the can was moving erratically and without any discernible pattern. I knelt down next to it, and using a Popsicle stick that I picked up off the ground, I lifted the edge of the can and looked underneath.

There was no solution under the can, only another mystery. I saw a large black beetle on his back, his six shiny black legs battling the crushing weight of the steel above him. He pushed and twisted, try to escape, but he was effectively trapped. I gently lowered the can back into place and stood looking down. The can again began sending its flickering SOS.

I wondered if this was part of the end of the world. How could that beetle get underneath a flattened tin can if he was upside down? It was a problem definitely beyond the capabilities of my eight-year-old brain. I was confused; was the bug under the can a sign? Was I too dumb to understand what was happening? The can kept flashing its coded signal and confusing me more.

Why me? I thought. *What did I do wrong today? Was this a test?*

That's when I understood. It came to me like a blinding flash. I did not understand the intricacies of physics or even how to spell the word, but I knew there was a way to solve this mystery. I picked up my right foot and squashed the can, the bug, and the problem, all in one giant stomp. And as I walked down that alley toward home, I smiled to myself. The end of the world was surely postponed.

The Shot Heard All Over Texas
by Hank Godwin

My younger brother Carroll and I knew we were going to get the belt from our dad, gentle giant that he was. He was six-four and quiet most of the time, but when Mom's anger moved to threats of being dealt with by our dad when he got home, he could put on a whooping if it came to that. This was the Sixties in the rural South, long before time-outs, standing in the corner, or even groundings. It was going to be a pure and simple, physical, teeth-chattering, backside blistering, loud screaming and crying spanking. In other words, there was no talking our way out of this one.

I was eleven, Carroll ten, and we had been home alone. I'm sure it had been my idea, as usual, to pull out our BB guns and do target practice in our bedroom, since I could convince Carroll to do anything that seemed risky or fun to his warped ego. It started with hanging our Punt Pass and Kick awards from the ceiling, awards we had won by beating almost every kid our age in Carson County. The hard, copper BBs ripped through them with the precision of a sniper's hit as we smugly applauded each other with our prideful eyes. Then it was time for a real challenge, something more suited for our obviously masterful skill level.

I'm sure it was my idea and I'm even surer that Carroll pulled the trigger on the now infamous shot heard all over Texas. We could see about a three-inch square of my mother's porcelain-faced kitchen oven from our bedroom. The shot would have to go from our bedroom, through our hallway, across the corner of the den, into the dining room, under the cabinets with my mother's good china, and travel about ten feet of kitchen before striking the oven door.

There was no discussion. Most of my crazy ideas that I gave my brother went directly from my spoken word into action within seconds.

I felt like we were walking the thirteen steps of the gallows as we eased out of our bedroom, down the hall, through the den and dining room, and into the kitchen to inspect our dirty work. We knew exactly what the outcome was going to be when our mom got home and spotted the chipped porcelain with the petite dimple on raw metal. We had to have a plan.

Carroll said we needed some padding. That way it wouldn't hurt as much. Yep, that was our plan. It is unbelievable to me today that I considered this a good plan. After all, it came from Carroll.

We quickly stuffed kitchen towels in our jeans and sat quietly in our room waiting for our parents to come home. I remember the mumbling coming from the kitchen and my father stepping into our room. He always waited to pull his belt off until he got in front of us. I'm pretty sure it was part of the overall punishment experience. We knew there was no turning back once the weapon was drawn through all the loops on his pants. A belt in hand and being mad was not a good combination for Carroll and me.

"Bend over," the words I hated to hear my dad say. Fifteen seconds and four or five licks into the spanking it was going really well for us. The towels were working great. Our plan should have included some fake screaming and crying because our dad pretty quickly assessed that something was wrong. I remember the sinking feeling as my dad lifted Carroll's shirt to see the towel sticking out of his pants. He disappeared for a few minutes into the den where I'm positive I heard laughing. However, creativity would get us nowhere. We had to complete our punishment. We took the next several licks on our bare behinds; raw leather on bare behinds.

We survived as we always did, our bond deeper. Several weeks later on one of our stops walking home from school, we decided to drop in on Mom. We needed two quarters for the soda fountain. We barely entered the lobby of the County Extension office where she worked before the giggles and jabs began to roll out of her co-workers mouths, "Have you killed any toasters today?"

We quickly pivoted and headed straight home, neither of us handling the embarrassment very well. Then I realized, thanks to our mom, that we were destined to become fairly famous in a multiple county area of the Texas panhandle. And all from a single incredible shot.

Hello, Brown Sugar!
by Sharolyn Jones-Taylor

Shortly after my sister and I began drinking our Jack and Cokes from our small Styrofoam cups, the nurse entered the room, checking on Daddy, asking if we needed anything. We answered that no, thank you, we were fine, and all three of us pretended she couldn't smell the bourbon floating around the room. Then she quietly left. It was just before Christmas, and Daddy was at the end of his struggle with stage-four lung cancer. My sister was uneasy about having this presumed contraband (presumed because I never actually saw a sign prohibiting alcoholic beverages at the hospice facility) in our possession, but I assured her that the nurses had better things to do than worry about our nightcap, as long as we didn't get rowdy. She continued to worry, though, expressing concern that we would be the first people ever to be kicked out of hospice. Again, I reassured her that we were probably not the first people to have a calming nip while holding bedside vigil, and that even if we were, there was no reason for anyone to have us summarily booted from hospice. I mean, this was the South, after all.

Being Southern, I am drawn, for reasons both culture- and pallet-driven, to the warm, loving liquid embrace of sour mash. Specifically, Jack Daniels. My friend Scott prefers Drambuie, but then he also uses words like "milieu" and "pedagogy" so, go figure. While he distributes his *bon mots* as though they were alms for the vocabularily poor, I prefer the simple things in life, both in my lexicon and in my libations. I love the tart burn that cuts saucily through the Coke and slides confidently down my throat, warming me from the inside-out. The taste of Kentucky bourbon is one of rebellion—of sass. It is a heady mixture of crass redneck, back room poker games and secretive, boozy southern belles, with a *soupçon* of old school white trash.

My daddy, like Jack Daniels, was full of both rebellion and sass. As a runty, but spirited kid, he once got revenge on a bully who repeatedly stole his lunch by carefully preparing a dog poop sandwich, then frosting the edges with peanut butter. Predictably, the bully stole his lunch, bit into the sandwich, and beat my daddy to a pulp. He did not, however, take Daddy's lunch again.

True to form, Daddy was an oddball even in that last week. Imagine my horror when his nurse, a smiling, middle-aged black woman, was greeted with, "Hello, Brown Sugar!" Mortified, I quickly told her that I was sorry, my face starting to heat up. I left the room in shame. Twenty minutes later, when I returned, that nurse was giggling like a schoolgirl, telling me, "I wish he was my daddy!" I think I mumbled something to the effect that she could have him. During that last week, he also invented a game he called "Eat My Shorts," the rules of which I won't go into, but it did entail flinging crumbs from his sweatpants and—well, never mind.

Daddy was a content Southerner. He had a ball cap that said, "American by Birth, Southern by the Grace of God." He was the kind of man who would hit you in the eye with a snowball, then tell you Democrats don't cry. The kind of man that women fell in love with, even after he was fat and bald and broke. The kind of man who would cheat on your mama, then slap his date when she bad-mouthed your mama. The kind of man who would pass gas in public and blame it on you.

And then came cancer. When it finally became clear that Daddy's organs were failing him and there was no real hope, my sisters and I made the heart-breaking choice to have him moved to hospice. I, along with one of my sisters, stayed with him there. In preparation for our stay, we went to his house and packed up some necessities—clean underwear, toothbrushes, and a T-shirt apiece. Before we left to return to the hospice, my sister grabbed the box of Ding-Dongs that Daddy had in the cabinet. And I grabbed the Jack Daniels.

As night fell, my sister and I were in our respective hybrid chair/beds, talking about everything from our childhood to funeral arrangements and paying Daddy's bills. Before long, feeling sorry for myself—for both of us—I padded down the quiet hall to the "Nourishment Room," retrieved a Coke from the refrigerator full of canned sodas, school-sized 2% milk, and Jell-O pudding cups, padded back to the room, and pulled out the JD. With a hushed reverence that is appropriate on such occasions, I mixed two drinks in small Styrofoam cups and produced two Ding-Dongs from our bag of provisions.

So we sat, in our pajama pants, each wearing one of Daddy's sweat shirts, drinking and talking into the night, both utterly exhausted but afraid to go to sleep. Afraid that Daddy would go and we would not know it. Afraid that we would awake to find him gone. Afraid of what it would mean to no longer have a daddy, even one like ours.

So we talked. And we laughed. And we cried. And we finally turned out the lights, and we talked some more.

Proposals

by Rex Robbins

And so we wait. I'm nervous, and really want to see how this turns out, but, Mary, my twenty-five-year-old daughter, wants to move on. In just a few minutes a young man's life will be laid open and hung out over a precipice. Mary seems bored. The thought crosses my mind—women really don't get it.

It's Saturday morning, and we are climbing the east side of Pinnacle Mountain in Central Arkansas—the hard side, the one with the boulder field stacked upward at a knee-wrenching slope. Only a few people are on the trail. Just before topping out on the south peak, we approach three young men sitting leisurely on rocks with a humongous video camera pointed in the general direction of the north peak which is about one hundred yards away.

Now this is a mystery. They have lugged this big expensive camera up the mountain, but seem to have no interest in the panoramic views from the highest point. The only thing unusual about the north peak, as far as I can tell, is a small splash of yellow, too far away to identify.

Puzzled, I look back at the guys. "There's about to be a proposal," one of them tells me.

Let's see. Proposal. Business. Money. I'm still confused.

"A marriage proposal," he clarifies with a tone probably reserved for those diagnosed with encroaching senility.

"Oh, that's cool. So are those flowers over there?" I point to the yellow splotch on the distant peak. He confirms that they are.

"Does she know?" I ask.

"We don't think so."

So it all fits now. The hopeful groom-to-be has chosen a mountaintop to pop the question, with fresh air and open sky, in front of God, three buddies and a few intrigued hill climbers. The proceedings will be filmed from a discrete distance using a camera with a powerful zoom lens. Flowers mark the spot. The guy must be a bit of a romantic, perhaps, not unlike myself. I proposed to my wife not far from here in a park overlooking Lake Maumelle on a starry night.

Climbing the last few steps to the top of the south peak, I suggest to Mary we stay and watch. We select a hard rock seat, with a view of the north peak, perched just above the film crew.

I recite for Mary a story she's heard before—the story of proposing to her mother. We can see the lake and so I point to the general location where it happened. Tucked away in a small cove off the lake, too far to see, close enough to feel. I remember the warmth of the moment, but also the tinge of fear that rejection, at least uncertainty, was still a possibility.

"It didn't go exactly as planned," I tell Mary. "I had no idea roses would wilt in one afternoon if tossed on the dashboard of a pickup truck. There was the lake and the stars were out, and something dead that smelled to high heaven."

The bad omens were not working in my favor. But thirty-one years of near-perfect marriage and three daughters later and now I am sitting next to my youngest on a rock that witnessed it all. Just as I finish the story I see a slender man in his forties climb up from behind us. I can overhear most of his conversation with the film crew.

His voice is huffy. "None of you were able to talk him out of it? It's not all that it's cracked up to be."

He climbs on up to the point where Mary and I are sitting. I can't resist poking at him. "So you wouldn't get married again?"

He is surprised by the question, but quickly recovers. "Well, this is the last time."

I'm guessing he's been to the well and drank the water more than once or twice before.

A few people come and go, but nothing is happening on the north peak. It begins to get cold and my daughter Mary is ready to head down. I resist for a few more minutes, but finally concede. Our plan was to hike down the west face, the easier side, and then circle back around the base trail to our car.

As we descend, we should pass the young couple on their climb up. I remind myself not to smile stupidly or issue any words of premature congratulations. Sure enough, just as we reach the saddle that separates the north and south peaks, a young couple crosses the trail in front of us and begin making their way out to the north peak. Mary turns and smiles, but is ready to continue down. Not me.

Even now, there is the possibility of this ending badly. It is not the most radical proposal in the world, but it is being witnessed—and filmed. I think of those videos my son-in-law talked about seeing on YouTube documenting ways not to propose marriage. "Don't put the ring in a food item" was the advice in one of the clips. The next image shows an X-ray with the ring inside the girl's stomach. Another clip was a broadcast of a professional basketball game. The girl has been lured to center court. The guy shows up, drops to a knee and presents a ring. The girl considers the question for a moment, whispers something to the guy and then runs off the court—alone. The TV announcer is not sympathetic, "Aww, he'll get over it in ten to twelve years," he says.

I have already given instructions to my daughters in case something like that happens to them. Have a heart. Act surprised, smile sweetly, and tell the guy, without moving your lips, "Yes, we'll talk la-ter."

I am nervous. Here on Pinnacle Mountain, things could go badly. What if the young man is rejected and decides that life is not worth living? I try to remember my scout training in high mountain rescue techniques. Actually, I never made it out of cub scouts. The dude is SOL.

For their part, the two seem calm and oblivious to our presence and the impending disaster I've created in my mind. They slowly work their way further out onto the rocky ridge, steep cliffs on both sides. We cannot hear anything they say, only a gentle wind through the trees. They walk up to the flowers. No visible reaction. Does she see them? Maybe she thinks the daffodils bloomed early this year. They walk a little further and stop. He takes her in his arms, then gets down on one knee. After a few moments, her hands go up to cover her face. Then she leans over, takes his face in her hands and kisses him. A lovely word, "Yes." More so when viewed in pantomime.

I breathe easier now, finally convinced the guy will not be jumping off the mountain. Funny. I don't know their name, never heard them speak a word. Yet, somehow they put a lift in my step. Maybe it comes from witnessing something positive. Maybe it is that I recognized a kindred spirit in the young man.

Mary and I start our way down the west side of the mountain—the side facing the lake. The water is barely visible through the trees. It is bright daylight, but I swear I can almost see the stars.

The Editor

by Darinda Sharp

I worked my way through the crowd, into a line of more than three hundred people to meet one of my favorite authors and get him to sign his latest book. It was October of 2009 and more than 1,500 captivated fans packed into a school auditorium to hear to him speak. David Sedaris had come to Little Rock, and I was there—front row, stage right.

I assumed he'd read from previous works. He had seven books and dozens of articles to his name, so he didn't have to search for material. My assumption was wrong. He treated us to some of his unpublished work.

One piece was from a forthcoming book of animal fables. In the story, several critters stood in an airport-like line grousing about unreasonable procedures and bureaucratic inflexibility. The counter agent, a black snake, refused to bend the rules. An argument ensued and ultimately, the duck walked away.

Something about the story bothered me, but I couldn't figure out exactly what. Was it one of the points of the story? There were several messages—some more subtle than others—about violence, racism, security, ignorance, and hypocrisy. Was one of the lessons hitting too close to home? I didn't think so, but I wasn't sure.

As I stood in line, waiting to meet this man whose words had been part of my life since college, the story continued to eat at me. He warned us during his talk that he always asks questions of people when he does signings. If we were going to pry into his life it's only fair for him to do the same, right? By the time I reached him it was almost midnight, and I had identified my aggravation with the story. I had my question ready, but he went first.

His question led us into a nice little conversation about Fayetteville—my hometown and the next stop on his tour. Then it was my turn.

"In the animal story, when the duck walks away, why does he walk away?" I said. "Why doesn't he waddle away?"

He looked at me, expressionless. "I don't know," he said.

I was afraid I might have offended him, so I kept talking. "It's just that you're typically so precise with your word choice."

He kept looking at me, but it felt more like he was looking through me. So I kept talking. I've never been one to get starstruck, but I've watched plenty of people become flustered and stupid when meeting an actor, singer, or politician. This time I was the flustered, stupid one.

"I thought there might be a reason that you chose—I, um. I was just wondering."

I finally shut up long enough for him to answer.

"I don't know," he said again, seeming to come back into the moment. "That's a very good observation."

"Thanks!" I said, beaming like a kindergartener who just got a gold star from the teacher.

Then, the unbelievable happened. He reached into his jacket pocket and fished out a little notebook. I'd read about this notebook for years. I knew what it was, and I couldn't believe I was actually seeing it. He opened the notebook and started scribbling.

"I'm going to change that," he said, still scribbling. He stopped writing and looked directly at me, "on your suggestion."

I thought I might faint on the spot. Now I can die happy. I just edited David Sedaris.

I pulled myself together, and managed to speak in a steady voice (I think).

"Thank you," I said. "It's nice to meet you. Please say hi to Fayetteville for me." And I walked off—no, I bounced off.

I could think of nothing else for several days. I eventually stopped boring my friends with the story, but everyone must have heard it at least three times before I realized I had become a broken record.

In early November of the following year, I was listening to NPR and heard someone reference a new Sedaris book. That has to be the book, I thought. It's been more than a year. It must be out by now. In fact, it was released in September. I completely missed it.

One question remained: Had he actually made the change?

I rushed to Barnes & Noble, found the humor section, and then the book. It was on the bottom shelf, so I squatted in front of the bookcase, and picked up *Squirrel Seeks Chipmunk* by David Sedaris.

Not bothering to move to a chair, stand back up, or even sit down on the floor, I flipped through the pages with reckless abandon, as if I was going to turn directly to the story, or recognize it on sight. I stopped. I needed a plan. I decided to start with the table of contents, but what was I looking for? It had been a year. I didn't remember the whole story, much less the title. Something about a duck, of course, and a snake.

Each chapter had animals in its title, "The Cat and the Baboon," "The Parenting Storks," "The Judicious Brown Chicken." Only one mentioned a duck, and only one mentioned a snake.

The duck tale came first, so I decided to start there, "The Turtle, the Toad, and the Duck."

Oddly enough, I didn't scan the story. I actually read it. Within three paragraphs I knew it was the one. I kept reading slowly. I enjoyed it the first time, so I knew it would be fun to let the story unfold as my memory caught up.

Then, there it was. I was so excited that I immediately sent texts to the kind souls I had exhausted with the story a year earlier.

Text 1.

New Sedaris book, p 27:

Text 2.

"Yeah, well, to hell with both of you," said the duck and he waddled off . . .

Text 3.

WADDLED!!!

I had to fight my impulse to squeal and jump around. Instead, I closed the book, stood up, walked directly to the front counter, and bought it.

Driving home, my mind drifted back to the euphoria of that October night. I can die happy. I just edited David Sedaris.

Then, a new question crept into my head. When I hit the door I went straight to my MacBook and started checking all the standard online sources for the answer to my newest dilemma. After half a dozen websites, I reached for my well-loved Oxford Dictionary/Thesaurus, and then the two writers' handbooks I keep beside it. Gaining confidence with each source, I became comfortable with the answer.

"Edit" is a transitive verb meaning: to prepare material (written, audio, or video) for publication by correcting, condensing, or otherwise modifying it. Edit is what I had done. I had been his—editor.

As I closed my laptop and returned the books to their shelf, my WJSAT folder caught my eye. This is where I keep the letters from places that have rejected writing submissions. It stands for "We'll Just See About That."

I leaned back in my chair and smiled.

Wrestling with the Blues

by Mare Carmody

When my phone rang Thursday, it was my friend Johnny Mac. "Do you wanna make some extra dough Friday night?"

I'd graduated with a B.A. in English the year before, but what paid my rent was a day job in a music store, and nights singing in bars. My mom couldn't understand why I didn't just move back home so I could get a real job, make money, and find a decent place to live. "Extra dough? Doing what?"

Johnny Mac was a guitarist and wannabe entrepreneur, and was often looking for a favor. "Singing at Norfolk Arena. There's this promoter guy who's booking wrestling matches there and he wants solo and duo musicians to play before the matches and maybe in between rounds."

"Yeah, right. Why would he want that?"

"It's cheap entertainment, and he's probably got a limited budget."

I was in desperate need of a space heater for my one-room apartment. Suddenly I was intrigued. "So like, how much?"

I called that afternoon.

"Reid Douthet." The voice was monotone and clipped.

"Um. My—my name is Mare and I play music here in town, and . . . "

Silence. I swallowed air and jumped in. "I heard you were looking for musicians to play at the Arena this weekend."

"Yeah. You have your own sound?"

I affirmed that I did.

"One hour, hundred twenty bucks. You gotta do some pretty lively stuff, no Joan Baez."

"I don't do Joan Baez," I said stiffly. Several years of bar music had toughened my repertoire considerably, and that last line was like a gauntlet thrown down.

"Be at the Arena by six Friday. First match is at seven, you gotta be ready to go."

I tried on six changes of clothes Friday before I gave up and wore what I'd usually wear to an average club gig: black Levi's, tight t-shirt, lots of eye makeup. What does one wear to a wrestling match, especially when you're part of it?

I pulled up in the fire lane at Norfolk Arena, a hulking granite tomb of a building, built some time in the 1940s when Navy enlisted men crowded in to watch the fights. I put on my flashers, got out the hand truck I kept with me, and started loading my small p.a. in.

Inside: gaudy amounts of brighter-than-natural light, booming echo, big wrestling ring in the center. At least it was warm in there, although there was also a definite scent of something like locker room. I felt my first true prickle of fear: what the heck was I getting into here?

I sauntered up to a man with a headset and a clipboard. He was about forty, built compact like he'd been a wrestler once, with tightly Bryl-creamed hair the color of lo mein noodles.

"Can you tell me where I'm supposed to set up?"

He sized me up momentarily, and then jerked his thumb at the ring. "That's where you're gonna be."

"In the ring? Couldn't I be like, next to it? In front of it?"

He looked at his watch. The unspoken message: take it or leave it.

I squared my shoulders. That which does not kill us will make us strong. After all, it wasn't something my parents had to know about.

I pushed the two long speaker columns of my p.a. underneath the ring, facing out in opposite directions. I connected the cables to the mixer and hoped the Arena's massive echo wouldn't turn everything into a sonic stew. I smiled at the ring girls in hot pants and high-heeled boots, holding placards with numbers for each round. And then I climbed onto the stairs, between the ropes, and up on the canvas with my microphone stand and guitar.

If you have never spent any time in a wrestling ring, you should know that the canvas bounces underfoot just as much as it looks like it does on TV. I edged toward the ring's center with my stand and guitar, feeling like I was on the deck of a ship, trying to balance my center of gravity somewhere between my thighs and knees. After I got situated and the Jello-y sensation eased up, I dared to look at the Arena seats. Not a sellout by any means.

Normally, I find someone in the audience and sing to them directly. But not this night. I hit the guitar strings one time, a bold, satisfying brawwwng that was absolutely huge, bouncing up from the speakers and spreading out to the sides of the Arena. For a moment, I had everyone's attention, staring at me: what on earth is that crazy girl in the ring doing? Then they all went back to their non-attention.

I inhaled deeply. *It's all or nothing now.* I'd tried to make a list of the rowdiest songs I knew, blues and rags and anything somewhat bawdy, so I started with "That'll Never Happen No More," and "Dust My Broom," and when I saw a glimmer of interest in the slack-jawed faces around me, I slid into "Hesitation Blues" and "Whiskey & Gin." What a power trip! My voice had never rung with such presence. The quivering canvas underfoot now felt like it was moving with me, adding to my swaying rhythm. I did five songs in a row without stopping. It wasn't like singing at D.B. Coopers, or Papa's Pub, any of my usual gigs. This, now, I could get used to.

"Man I love, stole from my best friend/That girl got lucky, stole him back again/You better come on in my kitchen, because it's gonna be raining outdoors . . . " Scattered anemic applause. I might hone a career as an ole blues mama after all.

But then things started fading just as fast. I tried "St James

Infirmary Blues," and "If I Can't Sell It, I'll Keep Sittin' On It," bending the notes, rolling my eyes when necessary, anything to get the song across. Despite how cold I'd been earlier, now there was a line of sweat across my hairline. I started glancing out of the corner of my eye, waiting to see someone make a guillotine motion across their neck, or some sign to let me know it was all over.

The song ended, and an ominous buzzing echo took over. Not a single clap, no glances from the ring folk. Over to the side, I noticed several wrestlers in warm-up robes, milling restlessly and jogging in place.

And then, incredulously, "Marilyn? Marilyn Carmody, is that you?"

I nearly wrenched my neck trying to locate the voice. And then, just as amazingly, I found it: my dad's best beer-drinking buddy, Walt Isaacs and his wife, Billie, about six rows from the floor. Nobody would call me Marilyn but my folks and their friends. Walt and Billie were grinning and waving at me like crazy, and I knew that was the end of my tough-girl showbiz career at the Arena. I gave my audience a sardonic salute and lifted my guitar from around my neck, preparing to exit the ring—just in time, it seemed, since the first match was ready to start.

"Is that really you? Wait till your folks hear where we saw you!"

I stood still and waited for my neck to be hugged, and life as I knew it to resume.

The Confession
by Jacob Craig

I was haunted by the thought of watching the other Catholic kids in my class stand up and take Communion while I sat in the pew with the teacher and the handful of Protestants. My legs started shaking up and down, knocking on the maple pew in the back of St. John's Catholic Church. I had to figure out what sins the others were confessing, so Father would think that I was ready for Communion.

Week after week, I had followed Dad through the wooden doors of St. Mary's Catholic Church, a sixty-year-old church in downtown Hot Springs with a turn-of-the-century facade. I had read and sung with everybody else during Mass while we watched Father work behind the altar.

The first time I did the whole Mass all the way through like everybody else with no mistakes, Dad bought me a brownie and a lemonade downtown.

I had started going to Catholic school in the first grade, and in the second grade, my class received instruction for our First Confession and First Communion. I paid attention to the instruction, because they told us that if we didn't, we couldn't get our First Communion. And before we got our Communion, we had to have our First Confession.

At home, Dad had asked me about the instruction while he pulled out pictures of his First Communion. His favorite was a picture of him and Grandpa on their front porch. Dad was in a white sport coat with black pants and shiny black shoes. Grandpa had his hand on Dad's right shoulder, and they had the same kind of reluctant smile with their lips closed and stretched across their faces into the corners of their mouths. I knew Dad wanted me and him to take a picture like that in front of our house. Before Dad put the picture up, he said, "We've got to get you a white jacket."

Father had arranged to lead religion class the day before the Confession. He said he was subbing for Ms. Clardy, and we all laughed. Father had stopped in sometimes, but it was never for the entire class period. And we never had his full attention. But on the day before our First Confession, he was completely focused on us.

Father was in his full dress coat, a black robe-ish garment that went down to the tips of his wingtip shoes and had a line of black cloth buttons down the front. Father looked like a saintly Fonzie in that outfit. Father adjusted his glasses on his head and folded his hands together:

"Tomorrow is your First Confession. It is a big deal. Before you can take the living flesh and blood of Christ, you have to confess your sins, and there is a certain way to do it. And you must do it right."

For the rest of the class, Father drilled us on the Act of Contrition. He ended the class when we started asking questions about whether accidentally killing someone counted as mortal or venial. He said that he was ready for lunch and that we were too.

As the line to the Confessional started winding down, my nightmare of missing my First Communion seemed possible. I had no idea what kinds of sins to tell Father to make him happy, so I decided to just make some up.

I used all of my sources —the *Home Alone* movies, the villains on Saturday morning cartoons, and a couple of stories from shows on *TV Land.* I started making my list in my head; I mouthed them to myself to practice, and when the confessional door opened, I felt ready.

The Confessional smelt like Dad's bathroom. Right in front of the door was the kneeler with the screen in front of it. I sat in the chair across from Father to show him I was brave and to figure out if I was passing or failing the test.

Father sat in his black suit and black dress shirt with his white collar and the green stole hanging from his neck to his knees. I sat down and crossed myself, "Bless me Father for I have sinned. This is my First Confession."

Father raised his head from the closed Bible he held in his lap and looked into my eyes, "Tell me your sins, my child."

"Well, Father, it is kind of long." His face stayed blank, and his eyes stayed bored.

"Go ahead." He had become a statue.

I ran down my list. "I lied, cheated, stole, coveted my neighbor's wife, and coveted my neighbor's goods. I killed some ants with a magnifying glass. I lied to my mother. I lied to my father and disrespected him. I took the Lord's name in vain." The priest's face stayed stone-still. I had to turn it up a notch.

"I burned down our neighbor's shed. I stole money from the grocery store." I was getting a reaction then. I pursued the task like a poacher after King Kong. "I punched an old lady. I kicked a cripple kid in the leg. I threw red paint on a crucifix." It went on like that, and his mouth dropped like he was watching a man swallow swords on a unicycle. Then, he closed his mouth and grinned.

"Is that all?"

"Yes, Father."

He opened his Bible, and he started reading the part that Jesus said about the golden rule.

He absolved me for my sins with the promise that I wouldn't do them again. I agreed. It sounded like a fair exchange.

"For your penance, I want you to say the rosary once for every person that you hurt. Say all the mysteries. By my count, you need to do it about thirty times. Let's make it thirty for safety."

I wanted to stop what was happening, but it was too late. That was just too much prayer.

But, if I 'fessed up to the lie, then I would have to do a confession for lying to a priest to the priest that I lied to. That was too much.

"Thank you, Father."

I shook his hand and left. I walked through the glass doors up to the altar. The church had gotten darker. Only me and a couple of other kids were still there. I knelt down and started praying.

"I believe in the Father almighty . . . "

"Our Father . . . "

"Hail Mary . . . "

"Hail Mary . . . " etc.

The noon sun rose and fell in the sky. The priest finished the confessions hours ago, and I was still kneeling at the altar praying. At one point, I sat on my heels. Father came out and gave me a brief lecture about physical displays of reverence to my Savior. I listened. I didn't want anymore "Hail Mary's." My knees started falling asleep and then they started hurting. I moved to a kneeler and kept going. A kid from my class came in and handed me my make-up work.

It was three o'clock. My mom was in the parking lot waiting for me. I started talking fast, talking in abbreviations. "Oh Mary, you are good. Help us. We are evil." "Our Father, it's your world.

Bring us Heaven. Amen."

I rattled through the last rosary at 3:14. I left the Church with my make-up homework, and I went to the parking lot where Mom was waiting in the car.

"Hey, sweetie. What took so long?"

"Nothing. I had to finish up some work real quick." I wanted to say that I had to ask the teacher about something, but the thought of one more Hail Mary was too much.

"So what did you do at school today?"

I buckled my seat belt and met her eyes in the rearview mirror. "Nothing."

She started to back out of her parking spot. "You always say 'nothing.'"

Dancing Around Daddy
by Judith Waller Carroll

It all started with Darktown Strutters Ball. It was 1956, and my sister was about fourteen. She and a couple of girlfriends got the idea to learn the Charleston for an upcoming Roaring Twenties dance. Much to my mother's disapproval, they had come over to our house with records and cranked up the Victrola in the living room. Mama flashed her usual warning look, but my sister ignored her and pushed back a couple of chairs to make room.

I hung on the sidelines, eager to join in, but with one ear cocked toward the back of the house where Daddy was reading a Raymond Chandler mystery.

Mama made it clear to us from an early age that once Daddy entered the "sanctuary of his home," as he liked to call it, he wanted things orderly, quiet and calm. She was as meticulous as a general in planning our evenings so that dinner was on the table at six on the dot, my sister and I were seated beside her with quiet voices and company manners, and the house was as still as a tomb the rest of the evening so my father could read in peace.

Then Darktown Strutters Ball started, and Sharon, Loretta and Myrna began to dance. Myrna was the bossiest of the trio, and since she'd been taking tap dance lessons at the Moose Hall for as long as we could remember, she was the natural leader. At Mama's insistence, the music was playing at the lowest possible volume, but it wasn't long before Sharon turned it up a notch.

I was drafted as Loretta's partner, and Pepper, our fox

terrier, who went everywhere I went, frolicked beside us. Mama, who loved music of any kind, soon joined us in the living room, dishtowel still in hand, tapping her foot and offering suggestions.

In an old photo album in our living room, there was a series of pictures of a much younger version of our father: holding an enormous trophy, playing tennis, a group shot with the debate team, and my favorite, Daddy doing the Charleston—arms flung out, legs askew, a look of pure joy on his face.

My sister and I would look at those old photographs with a sense of awe. This was a part of our father's life we knew nothing about. The photos we had on the shelf reflected the dignified man who went off with a briefcase every morning to teach eighth grade in a rural school about an hour away. He came home in the evenings, changed into slippers and a cardigan sweater, and retired to his study to read or correct papers, emerging long enough to eat supper and help us with our homework.

We'd see glimpses of the younger Daddy from time to time. Sometimes, without warning, he would burst into verse. He'd rock back on his heels, close his eyes, and recite a snatch of lines from Shakespeare or Tennyson or one of his other favorites. Other times he'd stop in his reading to point out an interesting word or turn of phrase. It might be snappy repartee from one of his detective novels or a lyrical line from Ralph Waldo Emerson. He loved to read. Words excited him, and he shared them with anyone within earshot.

"Listen to this," he would say, lowering his book and looking over the top of his glasses, and we would listen raptly, glad to be included in his private world of words and books.

But the young, carefree man dancing with such abandon in the photograph might as well have been someone else. Mama's brother Jack, for instance, who laughed easily, joked around with Mama and sometimes spun Sharon and me around the living room to one of the tunes on the radio. Uncle Jack's good humor was something we could count on. With Daddy, it was fleeting.

He could be smiling and laughing one minute, and the next thing we knew, something would rub him the wrong way and he'd blow like a geyser. His temper got him in trouble at school, too, but he was a gifted teacher and his students loved him, so the principal and other teachers chalked up his outbursts to the artistic temperament.

Thanks to Mama's diligence, we didn't glimpse Daddy's temper often. When we'd giggle uncontrollably or shove each other too vigorously while doing homework at the kitchen table, a stern look from Mama with a glance toward Daddy's closed door would usually get us to quiet right down.

If things got out of hand, Daddy would come out and intervene. Sometimes he'd put his hands on our shoulders and give us a fatherly lecture about the importance of getting along. Or he might try a teacherly approach, "Here, now, what's the problem?" Other times he'd shout, "Quiet!" from behind his closed door, or worse, come out and glower at us until we settled down. He'd walk back to his den, shaking his head and muttering, "Can't a man have any peace?"

Usually that would be the end of it, but if he'd had a bad day, our actions could be "the straw that broke the camel's back." When that happened, he'd storm out of the den, scoop his keys off the kitchen counter, grab his hat off the hook by the door, and head for the Atlas Bar down on Main Street.

Daddy had been sober since I came along, but back when he was drinking, a trip to the Atlas could mean he'd be gone for days. I guess Mama was still holding her breath. Even though he came back in an hour or so with his temper in check, Mama would sniff the air for a scent of whiskey and scan his eyes for signs that he was off the wagon, certain our bad behavior had driven him to drink.

We didn't mind the trips to the Atlas because it meant we could listen to the music we liked, laugh as often and as loudly as we wanted, bicker over the usual things sisters quarreled about and run around the house with Pepper nipping at our heels. Most of the time, our evenings were dull and quiet, our sibling rivalry confined to whispered battles behind the closed door of our shared room.

So that night, in our glee, we must have forgotten about Daddy reading in the back room. There we were, all of us whirling around, doing our own interpretation of the Charleston. Suddenly our father appeared out of nowhere and stood in the living room doorway.

We stopped in our tracks and held our breath. Daddy walked over to my sister, took her by the hand and started dancing.

It was a sight to behold. His feet moved like they were disembodied, keeping time perfectly, never missing a beat. Our portly father was as graceful as Fred Astaire as he nimbly executed the steps, spun around, bowed to my sister and then asked my mother to put down her dishtowel and take a spin around the room.

I recognized the look on his face. It was the same as the one on the young man in the photographs. Blissful, ecstatic.

Pure joy.

The Mercurochrome Files

by Rod Lorenzen

It is the winter of my older sister's discontent due to a nagging sore throat that seems to go on for weeks. Finally, my father intervenes. He seizes our old broom from a closet and plucks off one of the long, thin bristles. After taping a piece of cotton to one end, he anoints this with a household antiseptic product called Mercurochrome, then sticks the whole thing down into my sister's mouth and proceeds to swab the back of her throat with it until she gags. Ever the perfect little Pharisee, I stand there watching— fearful and unbelieving— and think surely my sister will die from such treatment. A few hours later, however, she is still with us and now seems to have been miraculously healed by the Mercurochrome.

Not long after this, when I am twelve and just the right age for being careless and silly, I somehow jab the points of my mother's good scissors deep into the soft tissue at the base of my thumb. Oddly enough, there is no blood pouring out and, to my amazement, I am able to look deep into the gaping wound. In a rational household, my parents would trundle me right off to the emergency room for a few stitches. My family is not rational. My father only glares at me and remains silent. I have seen this look before and know it well. It involves these two questions: "How could you do something so stupid?" and "How could we possibly be related to one another?"

As I ponder the wiring inside my thumb and wait for my mother to scream and yell, as she always does in a crisis (and sometimes even when there isn't one), she calmly suggests, "Put some Mercurochrome on it." I do as I'm told. But, to tell the truth, I am crestfallen. My hope to become the family's immediate center of attention for the next few days has vanished in a haze of apathy and disdain. Later, in the calm of gradual healing, I realize that the rightful celebrity of the moment was, of course, Mercurochrome.

It is our superhero, our emergency room and our panacea for cuts and scrapes, chigger bites, various aches, or any malady within dabbing distance. Most households in the U. S. possess a bottle of this mysterious red liquid. It works fast and promotes scarless healing and doesn't sting on open wounds like rival products. Ah, the miracles of Mercurochrome! It causes me to wonder at how Jesus of Nazareth worked his way through the Four Gospels on less. Some of my friends call it "monkey blood." In the summers, every other kid I know seems to be covered with it. These are our red badges of courage. Like the scars from our polio vaccinations, we wear them proudly.

But at this time, I can't know that somewhere in the future, a man in a lab will decide that Mercurochrome, which contains trace amounts of mercury, is unsafe. Though people swear by its curative powers, bureaucrats will ban it and manufacturers won't bother with trying to prove it's safe. By then, a new generation of antiseptics appear, and the trademark red of Mercurochrome will begin to fade fast.

There will come a time when you can't find it in Walgreen's or Kroger, although you can order it off the Internet from places outside the country. Actually, there will be a "mercury-free" version of it available in the U.S., but one has to wonder if it packs the potency and curative powers of the original, not to mention the aesthetic value.

And maybe the American Medical Association will lobby hard against good ole Mercurochrome just so doctors won't lose any business to a popular home cure. After all, using Mercurochrome is a procedure that defies the complicated business of medical billings and insurance filings and pharmacy visits, not to mention the very idea of government meddling in your private life.

But I am just a boy now and not terribly concerned about the future, which always seems to be such a long way off. And it is so easy just to have faith in everything—teachers, baseball heroes, home cures and a guy like Benny Craig. Benny is chubby and kindly and reads the sports news every night on Channel 11 in these early days of television. Sponsored by Colonial Bread, he is known as "The Colonial Bread Man" and dutifully wears his bread man's uniform and a policeman's hat when he is on television. He has his own simple prescription on how to make things better. "And remember, boys and girls," Benny intones at the end of each broadcast, "it never costs an extra cent to be a good sport."

On the very day my brother and I begin to build a tree house, the board we are nailing slips and the hammer smashes the nail of my left thumb, which immediately turns dark and bloody. I know exactly what to do. Fighting back tears, I rush into the house. As I gingerly dab on some Mercurochrome, I begin to have a glimmer that nothing will ever really quite assuage all of life's nicks and cuts. But, for now, Mercurochrome is always a good place to start. And, it pretty much always works.

Good Intentions
by Madelyn F. Young

I watched her enter the classroom. She hesitated, bit her lower lip and surveyed the other children. With a flip of her hand, she brushed straggly wisps from her eyes, then moved to an empty desk and took a seat.

As a student teacher, I was nervous, too. Noisy youngsters all around me chattered about things third graders find exciting on their first day back to school. With a firm voice, my supervising teacher called the class to order. The room hushed, and the 1958-59 school year began.

As the weeks passed, I noticed the child was quiet most of the time. She wore wrinkled, dirty clothing more often than not, and other children avoided her. Yet something about this student drew me to her. Perhaps it was her effort to learn. When I worked with a small group, she would be the one most eager to read or answer questions. She seemed to thrive on my attention, and that made me feel proud and useful.

An idea began to form in my mind, and it nagged me for several days before I discussed it with my husband. After our wedding in August, we moved into a small apartment two blocks from the college and elementary school. Now I was completing my senior year, and he taught in a city seventy miles away. He commuted on weekends and Wednesday nights. Could I work it out with the child's parents to let her spend the night with me on one of the evenings when my husband was gone? My plan included working with her on addition and subtraction and her spelling words. Mostly, I wanted to give her a bath, wash and curl her hair, and treat her as if she were my own little girl. I wouldn't mention that to her parents—only the schoolwork part.

I talked with my supervising teacher, who discussed my idea with the school principal. After receiving his approval, I talked with the child. Her excitement climbed as I thought it would. Since her parents had no phone, I gave her a letter to carry home.

The next morning her eyes sparkled as she handed me the note. "Momma says I can come home with you if I want to."

At the bottom of the page were a few words. "It will be all right." I marveled at her parents' trust, happy my plan would fall into place.

Tuesday morning, the child and I talked about how we would walk home together after school. She didn't bring a suitcase, or even a sack with a change of clothes, but I told her not to worry. "We'll make do," I said.

When we arrived at the apartment, I served her milk and cookies. Another child lived across the street, so I let her play outside while I prepared fried chicken and vegetables for supper. During our meal, she gnawed a drumstick down to the bone, reached for another, then devoured a thigh. Mounds of mashed potatoes and green beans disappeared.

We cleared the dishes and sat on the living room couch to work with flash cards. She cooperated for a while but soon tired, so I didn't push her. Besides, I was ready to begin her transformation.

We drew warm water into the tub and added bubble bath. I gave her privacy so she could undress and climb into the tub. When she was ready, I came in to check on her. Her thin little body looked small in the tub of bubbles, but her smile beamed.

"This is fun." She slid up and down from one end of the tub to the other. "It's so smooth."

I wondered if her tub at home was rough. Then it dawned on me—she might not even have a tub.

I gave her a washcloth and told her to use the soap and

wash all over her body. After several minutes, I helped her clean under her fingernails. Then I wrapped her in a large towel while the tub drained. Her hair needed a shampoo, so we drew more water and she stepped back in. Now we were both feeling more at ease. Careful not to splash water in her eyes, I laid her back so the warm water surrounded her face. Then I lifted her, applied shampoo and rinsed it as she lay back in the water.

I toweled her hair and body, then dressed her in a flannel "gown," one of my husband's old shirts with the sleeves rolled up. I combed her hair and rolled it on big brush rollers. She sat in front of the mirror, her eyes wide with expectation as I placed a dryer bonnet over her hair and turned on the heat. When we took down the rollers, her beautiful blonde hair fell in gentle curls around her shoulders.

"It looks nice," she said, grinning from ear to ear.

"I know." I smiled back at her. "In the morning, we may need to put a few rollers in it again before we get ready for school, but it will still look good."

She used a freebie toothbrush from the dentist. Then I tucked her into the makeshift bed of sheets and blankets on the couch. "Goodnight, sweetheart," I told her. "I'm going to get ready for bed now, too. See you in the morning." After a hug, she snuggled down.

I gathered her dirty clothes, carried them into the kitchen and washed everything at the sink, then hung her clothes in the bathroom and turned on the heater to dry them. I polished her worn and scuffed sandals. In the morning I would iron her skirt and blouse.

The next day we ate breakfast together, and then we got dressed. I gazed at the clean and happy child in front of me. My little Cinderella was now a princess. I was so eager to take her back to school. She was excited too, and she fairly skipped as we hurried along the sidewalk.

When we entered the classroom, several students were

already there. One of the boys looked up. I held my breath.

"Wow! What happened to Carolyn?"

All eyes turned in our direction. She stood there beaming. Before she could answer, another child spoke up. "She went home with Mrs. Young." With head held high, Carolyn walked to her seat.

After school the student teachers had a meeting. As I left the auditorium, I glanced at my watch. Almost four o'clock. A familiar figure bounded from around a corner.

I gasped. "Carolyn! What are you doing here? Did you miss your bus?"

"I want to go home with you again," she said, her face aglow with anticipation.

"Oh, sweetheart. I'm sorry. You can't. My husband is coming home tonight, and, besides, your folks haven't said you could."

The smile vanished, and she ducked her head. Frantically, I tried to think. Grasping her hand, I led her to the principal's office. With a heavy heart, I explained our predicament, and he said he would take her home.

Near the campus gate, an old car moved in my direction. I waited while it sputtered to a stop by the curb. An unshaven man, a tired-looking woman, and several blonde-headed children peered out through the open window.

"Are you Carolyn's parents?" I said.

"Yeah. Where is she? She didn't come home on the bus."

He scowled at me. I introduced myself and explained what happened. Then I apologized. "I'm sorry. She should be home by the time you get there."

The man frowned, muttered under his breath, then jammed the car in reverse and headed back the way he had come.

The next day I talked with Carolyn and repeated my explanation of why she wasn't able to come home with me. Her solemn eyes stared back, and she merely nodded. I gave her a hug. "Maybe we can do it again sometime," I said.

I watched her walk away. Her hair was straight, and her clothes—the same ones from yesterday—were wrinkled and dirty.

Blinking hard, I turned and hurried from the room.

Hunger

by Megan Riley

The heat drives against the insulation of the house. The Delta's 105° ambiance, breeze-free and so humid, the skin of bending knees gathers moisture like ditches. I escape with each hand's plunge into the dishwater and a box fan herding cold air from the living room's window unit into the kitchen. Two white-paned windows above the sink look out onto the front yard, reflecting a high tide of heat waves above black pavement. They seem to saturate his clothes, his four-foot-tall, seventy-five pound, decade-old frame. His face is reddened by skateboard overexertion—he walks into the house, slams the screen door, and shoots me the look. Uncertainty. Doubt. And at the same time, a familiar look that comes from years of putting up with it all. The red spreads across his ears and neck.

Our mother has somehow been buoying the household with her unemployment and his child support checks. Seven jobs in three years spanning two states: She is running out of options along with faith and the fortitude to explain what is going on. The bare cabinet shelves do the talking. Freshmen year at college was my first successful escape route and had been my safe haven of government sustainment. Scholarships and loans opened up my pocketbook potential and although it must be accounted for later, the now of two thousand dollars made me a beginner's millionaire. But summertime brought me back to this pathetic suction cup of a town where again, I face a reality they haven't been able to surmount.

"Drink some water, honey. You're face is red as a beet," I

say.

Then another look forms, a glare that seems to say "Really? You're coping with your third hangover of the week and you're telling me to drink some water?" But since he doesn't really know the reason I didn't come home until 3 a.m., why I smell like smoke and couldn't watch *Transformers* until we both fell asleep on the futon, the look can only signify "Oh please."

He puts his board down and goes towards the avocado cabinets for a glass. He picks up the small, blue plastic mug with foam letters spelling out "Noah" in a multi-color craze. I recall my matching "Megan" mug. Although nine years apart, we both prefer that vessel. The cup is too small to hold a substantial amount of anything, but the way the condensation gathers around the colored shapes, collecting until cold drops fall on the floor, toes, or jeans, the way the handle wraps around like a Fischer-Price embrace—it's comforting, and we cling to those blessings.

He laps up the tap water and I know I was right about the heat. A hundred in the shade is a lot to handle, even for Skinny Bones Jones, a nickname our grandmother coined for him. He refills his cup twice. His string bean arms glisten under the muted kitchen light as he draws in every ounce.

"I've got a trick you gotta see!" he says, after catching his breath from another gulp.

"Aww, yeah?" I reply, pretending to be aware of what he's talking about. The only wheels I'm interested in are the four out front, supporting the red four-door risk I take on the road every day. Gas leak one month, busted timing the next, none of the Cavalier's ailments are fixed but rather put off for another paycheck or some lottery ticket from some other state.

"Yeah, I was in Mrs. Wiles's driveway and I did two one-eighties!" he brags.

"So, would that make it a three-sixty?" I ask with a laugh, trying to stump him with numbers as to keep the rep of omniscient Big Sister intact.

"Well no! I did a kick step then did another one-eighty! Three-sixties are in the air, a whole circle," he explains in that vacant tone, just as his rude friends sound. It doesn't come naturally to him, though.

"Oh, okay honey."

I watch him open the cabinets, probably looking for some sugary sweet, gummy, glucose-infected package to satisfy his palate. As each door is opened then closed, I can sense his heart sinking, a heavy rock dropping towards the bayou bottom.

"Are you hungry?" I ask. I know the answer but ask anyway. He doesn't respond and instead, stands with the fridge door open, a huge no-no among house rules. Apparently, invisible dollars fly out with each second of stagnant fridge staring, though we both find ourselves guilty of such subversion, especially during the hotter days.

"Noah, are you hungry?"

"Yeah," he mumbles. He lets the fridge door creep shut, the seal inhaling deep the leaked cold air like some food safe, like there was food in there to keep safe.

"What do you want?" I ask, once again knowing the question is in vain, but not because I knew what his reply would be: The answer could not exist. His eyes begin blinking quickly and well up with tears. He sits by me at the plastic picnic table-turned-dining room table. As his body meets the bottom of the foldout lawn chair, he crumples up, his head plopping on the hard plastic, sweat droplets falling from his forehead and collecting into salty pools. He stares at them. He isn't depressed, suicidal, or suffering from some ridiculous diagnosis of dwarfed attention spans and tempers, but rather escaping. I watch the liftoff in his blue eyes.

"I dunno," he pushes out, his bottom lip pouting as he exhales a gust of frustration.

"Well, what sounds good? How about a grilled cheese? There's some shredded cheddar in there, I think."

"I had one earlier."

I get mad, but I don't show it. I understand that he doesn't understand. I can't say I have a firm grasp of it all either—the empty fridge, the empty plates, the empty wallets, the empty stares from behind black-gridded glass, nodding their empty heads like they know us, know the others sitting in the waiting room, know how it feels to lay in bed and pray for stamps that fill up fridges, that fill up stomachs. I'm sorry. You make too much money to qualify. When did fear become fair?

"Well, how about—oh look!" I throw out a phony exclamation as I find a can of generic raviolis. "How about these?"

"Mmm . . . uh-uh, I don't really like 'em."

I knew this. C'mon, Big Sister, think. How can I make him give in and eat these masses of dough smothered in a faux-meat sauce?

"Well, I can put some of that shredded cheese on 'em! And, oh, look, there's some butter! I can make some buttered bread? Sounds pretty good, huh?"

He raises his head from the table, the sandy brown buzz cut leaving his swollen eyes exposed. He looks like such a big boy with his bowl-cut gone, left at the foot of the barber chair at the beginning of summer. I want to cry, but I can't. It's his turn.

"Okay," he answers. A moment's silence falls while I look for the can opener. Avocado drawers scrape and the box fan hums a familiar tune, filling our heads, comforting us in the invisible cradles we wish we could crawl into, where we can cover our heads in blue and pink blankets and know nothing else. I find a container big enough for the family-size can, grind the metal open, and dump the dough ball bowl into the microwave. The beepbeep beepbeep echoes sharply in my ears and as hands find the butter tub, I hear the stretch pullrip of his sweaty skin being released from the tablecloth. He lifts his head up high enough to meet my eye.

"Do you want some?" he softly asks. I turn around with the empty can in my hand, damp palms wrinkling the purple label, and look at him, his filthy brow, those blue eyes.

"Sure, honey." I turn my body sharply right to hide a quivering smile.

I grab two big serving spoons for the dramatic effect of abundance. And as we feast on our stale buttered bread and scrape at the burnt raviolis stuck to the side of the big floral bowl, I know we made it. Lunch—a small victory, yes, but a victory it was. After a few hours, digestion will set in and the demanding rumbles will overtake our bodies again, but for this moment, we can sit in plastic chairs at a plastic table eating plastic food and feel fleshy, full, and free.

In This Our Last Act as Children

by Jeremy Harper

During high school years, my brother Josh and I earned our gas money as lifeguards of the local swimming pool. It was a dull and banal duty, never punctuated with a single moment of excitement. Not until that one afternoon which found me snapping the padlock shut at closing time, and I noticed my brother out on the parking lot, the trunk of our shared car opened, and a small assemblage of teenage boys milling.

"This is a mortar," I heard Josh say as I made my approach. "It fires these."

From my vantage point, I couldn't see what "these" were, but the enthusiasm expressed by my brother's audience could not be denied.

"Shoot one now!" said one boy, a twelve-year-old punk with a lifetime of punking still ahead of him.

I pushed my way inside the circle. Piled inside the car trunk, a colorful cacophony that resembled the crumpled body of a circus clown, was what appeared to be hundreds of dollars worth of fireworks.

There were Roman candles. M-60s. Bottle rockets. Six-ounce rockets. Eight-ounce rockets. Twelve-ounce rockets. Whistler batteries. And the before-mentioned mortar tube.

It was like the car trunk of Ares, but only if the Greek god of war had been placed in charge of Chinese New Year.

"Yeah! Fire it!" gushed a second boy. I saw what was in Josh's hands: a box of not-wrapped-carefully-enough cherry bombs.

Josh thought about it for a second. "Okay."

My brother set the mortar on the thinly graveled surface of the parking lot, taking some measures to insure that it was level. Next he dropped one of the cherry bombs into the tube. He fished his lighter from the hip pocket of his shorts, hunkered down like an Apache, and he lit the fuse.

Everyone retreated several steps as the spark marched up the fuse and disappeared inside the tube.

POOOMF!

The projectile was hurled into the sky at frightening velocity, penetrating the atmosphere with a splendid swoosh. When it had achieved an impossible altitude, the cherry bomb exploded, generating the type of racket only teenage boys and munitions experts fully appreciate.

"Hooo-yeah!" screamed somebody. "Do another one!"

Josh flipped the lid shut on his cardboard box of cherry bombs. "No. I'm saving these."

The audience scattered to their dinners, or to "Knight Rider" and Nintendo game consoles.

I surveyed the trunk once more and the explosive power contained within. If my brother had arrived with a trunk full of ninja stars, it would have been only half as cool.

"How much did you pay for all this?" I asked at last.

Josh smiled. "About a hundred and sixty dollars. The mortar was fifty."

That was a lot of coin. I looked at the mortar. "I don't know if you'll be allowed to use that."

Josh shrugged. "I even bought a new bag to carry it all in," he said. He pointed to a green duffle bag. "It's my War Bag."

My eyes passed across the packages of rockets. "You're going to take off somebody's head."

"Oh come on."

The pebbles crunched like breakfast cereal beneath our tires, and I saw that Josh and I were not the first to arrive at the gravel pit. Several cars were already parked on the scarred swatch of land scratched upon the rim of a valley, no longer in use for extracting gravel but still endlessly useful—essential, even—to eighteen-year-olds. A familiar blue truck had its doors opened.

Guns n' Roses blared from the speakers, the guitars screaming like acoustic battle axes cutting the wind.

"Kyle's here." I cut the engine. I knew most of the guys well. Classmates. A few were younger. I gave them a nod before punching Kyle on the arm. "You ready for this?"

As usual, Kyle churned with limitless energy, as though his body had cracked the secret of fission. He nearly inhaled an entire Marlboro in one breath.

"I heard Josh bought, like, two hundred dollars worth of fireworks!" he said, cutting to the chase. "Dang, I think I spent about thirty bucks."

Josh popped open the trunk. "I'm just trying to keep up with Bert," he said. Everybody began to crowd around. A low murmur erupted.

"What is that? A mortar?" said Kyle. Josh nodded.

"Are you trying to take somebody's head off?"

Six months earlier, it's cold and damp and my brother is on fire.

It's New Year's Eve, and somebody had casually mentioned a bottle rocket war a couple days before. Like anything that is reckless and foolish, this sounds like an excellent idea. And for some reason, it sounds safer than shooting each other with BB guns.

Josh and I purchased several grosses of Black Cat bottle rockets, and we believed we were holders of a powerful arsenal. However, it was clear early in the war that Josh and I had brought a knife to a gunfight. While bottle rockets were difficult to control and unpredictable in many facets, the Roman candle struck terror in those to which it was all too easily aimed. While I struggled to ignite a pack of bottle rockets, my opponents simply pointed laser-hot marbles of flaming terror in my direction.

Meanwhile, Josh and a few unfortunate Confederates had taken position it what at first seemed like a formidable bunker. It was a small knoll of gravel, with a depression cut from its crest so that it resembled a foxhole. But what seemed impenetrable was, in actuality, quite easy to toss a hot pack of firecrackers into.

Furthermore, there was no place to retreat or to fan out. Josh's camp glowed the entire evening, their cries of dismay punctuated with frequent screams of pain and rage. At one point, Josh's sweatshirt caught fire.

Josh would not forget his defeat that New Years Eve. In fact, he would replay the disaster inside his head for months afterwards, identifying tactical mistakes and developing improvements to plans of attack. When it was suggested that another war be raged on July fourth, Josh was more than game.

With a sliver of awe, we watched Josh extract rockets and cherry bombs from his green War Bag.

"He kind of took this seriously, huh?" said Bert. I nodded.

An hour of daylight still clung to the sky, and nobody wanted to declare war until nightfall. Josh ignited a salvo of cherry bombs to pass the time. With time to kill, I found a package of eight-ounce rockets, and I ripped them open. I admired the rocket's heft, liking its compactness, its explosive purpose. It felt dangerous.

I dumped one rocket into Josh's mortar cannon.

It was gone in an instant; a sizzle of sparks and a nearly transparent tendril of smoke.

Approaching the speed of sound, the rocket zipped past the boundaries of the gravel pit and disappeared deep into the tree line. I decided not to launch any more rockets.

Unlike the war on New Year's Eve, there were now girls in attendance. They leaned against the grill of Bert's truck, drinking cans of Coke and discussing the things that are important to girls. A couple of the boys had begun flipping bottle rockets at one another. I watched Kyle grab a Roman candle and unleash a barrage of neon horror upon the bottle rocket tandem. Josh and Bert smoked cigarettes, the War Bag at their feet. It bulged with finger-blasting goodness.

Kyle sprinted from out of the woods, his eyes wide and wild. He carried a spent Roman candle in one clenched fist. "The woods are on fire!" he yelled.

Sure enough, a serpentine wisp of smoke flittered lazily into the hazy sky. I thought of the rocket I had launched, sizzling into the trees. The girls darted into a dusty Grand Am.

"Where are they going?" I asked nervously. Kyle waved his hands. "They're getting the fire department! Let's go!" He disappeared like a madman into the trees, and we followed him.

By the time the fire engine pulled into the gravel pit, the fire was nearly extinguished.

The only evidence that remained was a blackened patch and a few stubborn lisps of flame. A mustachioed fireman handed Kyle a shovel.

The flames stamped out, we waited anxiously for our punishment. Would it be imprisonment? Indentured servitude? Or perhaps a discreet, gravel pit beating?

"Well, I guess you boys can go back to your firework display."

Long after the fire engine had vanished up the gravel road, we remained stunned by disbelief. We had set the woods on fire. Recklessly! The fire fighters hadn't even confiscated Josh's War Bag.

We divided into teams. Remembering his past failure in the bunker, Josh positioned his comrades beneath a lone, scraggly pine tree that some gravel miner had failed to remove. Soon the frequency of bottle rockets and Roman candle discharges increased. The heat of the day evaporated and gave way to the Oriental fire of explosions.

The dusk drew more weight. I was a considerable distance

away. Yet I could see the shadowy figure of Bert lumbering towards Josh and his cohorts, who were exchanging candy-colored fire with a third party. Bert withdrew his cigarette lighter, and he lit a crackling ball —a ten-cent plastic marble that emitted a great deal of white sparks. He tossed it.

The crackling ball bound past my brother and came to a rest inside his War Bag.

The War Bag didn't explode all at once. There were intervals of seconds when nothing happened at all, and then an ear-thumping burst or a streak of neon that would carom off the rocks and rip past our heads. Nearly five minutes expired before Josh's unscheduled show came to a close, leaving only a smattering of chuckles in its wake.

"That was about two hundred dollars worth of fireworks," I offered.

"And my new duffle bag," Josh added.

"The tree's on fire!" somebody shouted, and he was right. The skinny pine that Josh and his crew had made base was suddenly an arrow of flame.

We suspended our war to better appreciate the significance of the occasion. The summer was fading. The age in which we lived was disappearing. And a tree that had somehow missed the bulldozer was now felled by the foolishness of youth, in this our last act as children.

L-O-V-E

by Krystal Suit

The babysitter tells me that I'm a Mommy's girl. I think about this as I help Mom get ready for work in the morning, as she moves about the house unsmiling and silent, but for a soft "Thank you, luuk," when I hand her a shoe.

Remembering the time that she taught me to spell "love," I feel the brown carpet beneath my knees, cool glass under my forearms, the pencil in my hand, and I see the white spaces I haven't filled yet, the almost-letters that I've attempted. Over the sound of the television, I hear the foreign-but-familiar accent of Momma's words as she asks, "What you doing?" And steeped in my efforts, I tell her that I am writing. I imagine her blinking, even more skeptical of my ability to write than of her own, as she had never learned and I had yet to be taught.

Nevertheless, she asks, "Can you spell 'love'?" And thinking about it, I nod. Then I begin to string my almost-letters together, weaving thoughts of love into their shape, willing them to say "love." But she stops me and says, "No, luuk, not like that," and slides the sheet across the table. I place the pencil into her open palm, and she writes the letters L-O-V-E, slowly, in all capitals. When she offers it back to me, I shrug, telling myself that my way is just different.

I think about the time that I jumped feet-first into a pile of fire ants, even though Dad warned me that they would bite. Again I see them march up my long socks in neat rows that amaze me even as they bite my ankles, my calves. Then my shrieking overpowers the sound of Daddy's lawn mower, and he jumps off, yelling for me to go to the water hose. As he sprays my legs, half of me thinks that he is a genius. The other half observes that my socks and shoes are getting wet.

When he shuts the hose off, the first thing he says to me is, "You didn't believe me, did you?" And I remember that the reason I jumped was that I wanted to know what a bite felt like. I pinched my arm to see, but it didn't hurt, and I concluded that the only way to find out was to jump.

The babysitter told me once that I'm a Mommy's girl—but when Mom leaves, I do not stop to think about it. Mom tells me that she'll be gone for a year, to work for her friend in Oklahoma. I know that this is important, that nothing will be the same, but it is hard to feel the things that I have never jumped into. When she tells me, I shrug.

But at the airport, I feel the anxiety begin to bite at my insides. At every check point, on every subway ride, in every waiting area, I think that now is the moment, now is the moment that she'll be gone, now is what it will feel like forever, until they tell me that it isn't, that she isn't going yet, and there is one more place to go—until there isn't, and they cannot stop my cheeks from tingling, my nose from burning, my eyes from swelling, because now is the moment.

The house is bigger, quieter. At night I hear the rumbling solo of my father's snores. I sleep because I am afraid of the dark. Over the phone, I tell Mom that I love her, because that is all I know to say. When Mom sends me birthday cards, they always say "LOVE MOM," in all capitals, and the letters of the words make me think of the time that I tried to teach her how to read and write, but she did not try to learn, because she felt unhappy here, and she does not like when I try to teach her.

I think that Mom will not come back. I do not keep track of time. When I look at the babysitter, I want to tell her that I do not think I'm a Mommy's girl anymore, or if I am, I am a poor one.

One night, I dream of my mother's broken voice resounding in my ears as she cries that her daughter does not love her.

The echo leaves a biting in my throat, a burning in my chest. And when I awaken, I know that I will always remember the sound of her loneliness reverberating in my mind.

In the wake of my dream, my mother calls—and I speak warmly to her, carefully filling our white spaces with the vast love and affection that I feel strongly. I know now that she is human because she makes mistakes—and I love her because that is all she wants. What matters is that she is my mother as I am her daughter, in this moment as in all the moments that pass.

The Head Bone is Not Necessarily Connected to the Neck Bone

by Evelyn Menz

I was in Switzerland with my husband, prancing around one of those spas where bathing suits and towels are optional cover-ups. I took my original body on a tour, motivated by recent circumstances to take this opportunity while I had it.

On Groundhog's Day in 1999, a caller said there was good news and bad news and which did I want first? A neighbor, over for a look at a deck renovation which was later described as being built by Decks R Us, sensed something private was being shared and motioned she was leaving. I yelled after her through a cupped hand, "I have breast cancer." She didn't stick around for the good news. Oh, well. My husband, David, and my childhood friend, Cappy, were on their way to be with me. As we leaned against the counters in the kitchen, they sipped their glasses of wine while I gulped mine and said, "Yep, it's cancer but it could be worse." They stared at the floor through teary eyes.

The trip to Switzerland was not what the doctor had in mind as preparation for treatment because after an excision biopsy, in addition to a surgical oncologist, I needed an oncologist for chemotherapy and a plastic surgeon for reconstruction. I was shocked. Who were these people talking about?

This was an emergency because I had a plane to catch.

David and I called our motorcycle friends; the wife had battled breast cancer herself and knew the perfect surgical oncologist. We delayed their supper for an hour or so. The survivors gave us wonderful advice: no whining. Next was a best friend who had a best friend who was an oncologist, who advised, "You'll be fine but don't get an implant; they're up here or down there."

My niece, Erin, had a friend whose brother was a plastic surgeon. He had the bluest eyes and I'm sure his tan was from the sun on an exotic beach. He was very professional. I was not. While I gazed into those blue eyes, I asked, "Do you think my insurance would cover a face lift as well as breast reconstruction?" He answered, "Now, Evelyn, our first concern is to get rid of the cancer." Oh, that again.

I stayed true to myself and told my story to the painter, the postman, and the people who noticed the grayish complexion and the missing hair. David said my very big wig made me look like Conway Twitty because I could never keep the thing straight. "Find the points, Evelyn," he would say. From then on, I left it at the house.

Before I knew it, my good friend, Diane, asked, "Who appointed you poster child for the cure for the fight against breast cancer?" It was show and tell.

We decided on a TRAM flap reconstruction, which means the abs are tucked under an apron of skin, into the breast cavity where the breast tissue has been removed. THEY CAN DO THAT. These doctors are great at rearranging things so that the result isn't bad. Sometimes they can lift those babies to the moon. It's a miracle.

Going through chemotherapy was tolerable because of kind and experienced nurses. When asked about it I replied, "Nothing to it. It's a great excuse for going out to dinner, getting flowers and notes, taking naps and receiving family heirlooms early." Survivors wheeled through the driveway to drop off a goody of some sort, waved through the window something about a meeting or a tennis game that was waiting for them, let me know I would be there soon.

Hats, scarves, bad wigs, and nausea. A friend let me throw

up in her car. My hair grew out to look like my brother-in-law's, whose mane David always coveted.

A few years ago I went to France with two survivors: friends I had made through this experience. We played the cancer card and got in first class going over, prayed for forgiveness in a beautiful cathedral, and laughed and joked about our odd number of "boobs" for which we were grateful. I said, "This reminds me of the time I took the original girls to Switzerland. I don't know which trip was more fun."

Knock-Kneed

by Graham Gordy

You can't talk about who you are and where you come from until you understand who your dad was and who your mom was. And I'm not sure you can truly understand who they were until after they're gone.

My dad asked me to go outside and throw a ball around one day. A football. This might've been less surprising had I not been sixteen, he sixty-eight, and had he ever asked me to throw a football around before. My mom was out of town, and he was clearly seeing this as an opportunity to make up for something we hadn't done when we probably should've, ten years before.

It's not that my dad wasn't an athletic guy. He had been, I think. But he was retired now. Retirement, I suppose, being a time for reflection between all those *Matlock* reruns. As for me, I was gawky and narrow, with a big mouth of teeth. If someone had referred to me as pubescent, I would've considered it lavish praise. Emotionally, I was a distressingly tender thing. Painfully aware of my father's age, embarrassed that he wasn't like the other dads, but also living in fear of how quickly he might be gone from me.

So I took him up on the offer. This would be one of those beautiful moments I could remember when he was gone.

But there's nothing Kodachrome about liver spots, or grey, hairy arms, or translucent skin. And there are no Kodak commercials based on a quickly developing argument about someone's throwing technique.

"You gotta follow through on your throw more."

"Get your feet set."

"Get your elbow up higher."

I stopped, seething all too quickly, tucking the ball into my side. "I'm having trouble taking direction from a guy who throws like a girl."

"I don't have full range of motion in my shoulder!" he snapped back.

We went back inside. So it seems to go with sixteen-year-olds and their fathers.

This wasn't our first fight about things athletic. When I was eleven, I'd asked for a basketball goal in our driveway because I wanted to try out for our middle school team. Never one for numbers—or accuracy in most tasks for that matter—Dad "eyeballed" how high the goal should be. I actually went back and measured it years later. A regulation goal is ten feet. Dad put ours at a solid ten feet, eight inches. All the neighbor kids were utterly baffled as to why I was the Reggie Miller of west Conway while in front of my house, yet, in try-outs, every shot I put up hit the backboard at least half a foot above the rim. And so went my otherwise-assured career in the NBA.

It was events like these that colored my opinion of my father at the time. A typical teenager, I was having all sorts of crises—the existence of God, of justice, of romantic love—but if there's one thing I felt certain about, it was that my parents were complete imbeciles. I loved my dad. I mean, this was the man on whose lap I fell asleep every night until I was eight years old. But a pretty big gulf can grow between eight and sixteen.

Sixteen was also an age in my life when I was particularly wanting for identity. And why wouldn't I be? All jutting elbows and concave thighs, the idea of escaping into someone else seemed pretty appealing.

As far back as I can remember I was a Zelig, able to take the shape of my surroundings. I was a young actor, but a young mimic more than that. Like a politician, suited at the podium but with sleeves rolled up at the barbecue place, my southern accent was on an "as needed" basis and my inflections changed according to whom I was speaking. As for talents, my most marketable skill was that I was a smartass. I was a good one too. So much so that, in my sophomore year in high school, some senior football players asked me to come along with them on Friday nights and pick fights for them. I wish I weren't serious.

Up to then, my social life was fledgling at best. My best friend, Will, was a year younger than me and we spent our Friday nights foisting horrible practical jokes on people we either liked or didn't.

It being Conway, Dixie Flags were as ubiquitous on trucks as the cartoon Calvins pissing on Ford, or Dodge, or Chevy, take your pick. Will and I weren't educated per se, but we knew enough that the artifacts of a lingering Confederacy frustrated us and became our adolescent *cause célèbre*. So we removed them. On Friday nights, these trucks would gather in a couple of parking lots in town. Mulletted owners would open their tailgates and drink beer; all the while, Will and I would be under them, crawling from truck to truck, our Phillips-head screwdrivers in hand, removing their Rebel relics. At last count, I think the collection in Will's closet was up to forty. My most prized came from a truck that had a giant New York Yankees sticker on the back window. Apparently, the owner didn't see the contradiction. North and South—unified at last on a late-model Silverado.

But it was my first year of high school now, and suddenly, I was invited into a group of influential guys where I could do the two things I loved most: entertain and incite riots. It was simple really. They would drive up to a car full of other guys. I would lean out the window, mock their appearance enough to trigger a fight, then I would stay safely in a locked Bronco while my two hundred-plus pound confidantes would bludgeon the poor marks into oblivion.

One night, after a particularly triumphant round of this, these seniors invited me to a party. They had a weekend ritual of taking a forty-ounce of Colt 45 or Olde English malt liquor in each hand. Then they would have someone else wrap the bottles and their hands in Saran Wrap so you couldn't do anything but tink, tink them together. The rule, then, was that you couldn't get anyone to remove the forties until you finished them both. Now, I wasn't good at math, but even I knew that eighty ounces of beer in my juvenile, one-hundred-sixty-pound frame wasn't going to end well. But I forged on. And I drained them.

Considering the majority of my drinking to this point consisted of finishing my parents' friends' drinks after parties, I was at this point, to quote my father, "knee-walking, pecker-waving drunk." Yet I somehow found myself in line with my new friends at the keg waiting for more beer.

"Keg's tapped out," came a voice at the front of the line. There was a chorus of groans. "This sucks!" said one of the football players I was with.

In front of us in line were three longhaired rednecks. The group started dispersing. Wobbly, slurring, and full of Dutch courage since I was getting used to traveling with the Conway Wampus Cat's offensive line, my task became clear.

"Yeah, and if that's not bad enough, just take a look at these guys. I mean, just as human beings." The room went completely silent. In my mind there was a record-scratch but we were into the era of CDs by then so I guess that's impossible. My football-playing friends were the first to burst out laughing, then the rest of the room followed. The three rednecks approached me.

"What'd you just say?" the biggest of them asked. No turning back now, I looked at the back of his head, flipping his hair. "Sweet Kentucky Waterfall you got goin' back there. Achey-Breaky-Big-Mistakey." Another big laugh from the room. The redneck's jaw tightened and his eyes didn't move from mine. Then, one of my senior guardians leaned in to me softly and whispered, "Duuuude . . . those guys are big." And then he laughed. And then he, and my other defenders, left the room.

In that moment, any number of lives took a different direction, but mostly just mine. Having never been one to run from a fight, I stood my ground. Then I realized that I'd never been in a fight, so I ran. Out of the kitchen, through the living room, jumping the couch.

I made it to the driveway before the biggest of them caught me. His buddies needed not join in. His two punches landed swiftly. Blood filled my mouth. I don't remember hitting the ground, but I know I didn't start there. The rednecks yelled a couple of taunts, then got into their truck, their headlights shining on me. Through the front windshield, I could see the outline of a large, inverted New York Yankees emblem on the back window as they backed away and then took off. I looked at the front license plate. Empty. I managed to smile a little to myself . . . and then I bled more.

The football players were nice enough to take me home that night, and even apologized for not stepping in. I was still so drunk I could barely walk through the front door, then made the bad decision to take a seat on the couch even though my dad, a book open on his lap and ESPN playing, was asleep in his chair across the room. I leaned my head against the arm of it and my eyes began to close when he sputtered awake and looked at me.

"Son? . . . Son." He looked closer. "Did you get in a fight?"

"Lil' bit," I mustered.

"Are you drunk?"

"I'm sorry, Dad. I'm sorry." My eyes closed again. I started drifting off to sleep.

Then a strange thing happened. I felt two gangly arms lift me up. Torn rotator cuff. Restricted range of motion, and this sixty-eight-year-old man picked me up, Pieta-like, as if I were eight years old again, and carried me a good fifty feet from the living room to my bedroom.

As he carried me down the hall, I muttered, "I . . . I don't know what I'm doing most of the time, Dad."

"That's most of us, Son."

He put me in my bed and pulled the covers up. It was as close to falling asleep curled up on his lap as I'd done in almost a decade.

"Little fatherly advice?" he asked.

I managed a half-grin back.

"You can't grow up in one night."

Then he kissed me on the forehead, said, "I love you," and turned out the light.

That night, despite whatever distance, I understood better who my dad was. He treated me like a man, even if I was just flailing toward being one.

Bird Cage

by Margie Tubbs

Pete's cage in the dining room is set atop a hand-made china cabinet purchased used in the 1920s. I can't see him unless someone lowers the cage or I retrieve Mother's stepstool from the kitchen.

"Put him down here," I beg, jumping in the air for a glimpse of yellow-green feathers.

Jacky, my older brother, lowers Pete to the table as I watch his bright swatch of chest feathers grow from the size of a nickel to a fifty-cent piece. When he is eye-level, Jacky reaches inside the cage and places a small plastic car on a narrow wooden slat. Pete tucks his head and gently nudges the car with his curved beak until it rolls off the end. "Come on back. Pete won't hurt you!" he repeats in his nasal voice until his car is repositioned for another roll down the ramp.

I laugh as if I have never seen the trick before. "Come on back. Pete won't hurt you!" I mimic. "Mama, why don't you teach Pete something new?" She sits on the couch studying a book of crochet patterns.

"I'm working on it. It will be a surprise," she says, slightly curving her lips into the knowing smile that usually substitutes for an answer.

"Gotta put him back now," Jacky says, lifting the cage to its spot about six feet off the floor. "You can see him again later." As I had felt Pete's loneliness recede during the brief moments when that little car was under his control, I can feel it slowly returning now.

"You're crying again," Jacky says.

"Just seems unfair to keep Pete locked up there all by himself." He wipes my face with the tail of the blue plaid shirt that Mother made him.

"When's the last time you got out?"

"Out of where?"

"Here. When's the last time you went anywhere?"

"Tent church every Sunday."

"Is that all? Have you ever been to a drive-in movie?"

I give him a blank stare. "I don't even know what one of those is."

"Get your shoes on. We're going."

"Not with her." Daddy has just left his shop and is standing inside the kitchen door.

He brushes his sweaty khaki shirt, and sawdust falls onto the floor. "She's not leaving this house. You can go out whoring with your pretty boys, but she's not going." Daddy had cut off half his pointing finger in a saw, but he shakes what is left toward me.

On the couch, Mother vigorously crochets pineapples for a few seconds and then stops, looking over her glasses, her needles forming a V. She challenges Daddy with her stare.

"Just keep on wiggling that thread," he shouts. "Or better still, slither over there and coil up in the corner."

It was just last week that he threatened to kill himself and took the .22 pistol into the woods.

"Why aren't you stopping him?" I screamed to Mother.

"He won't do anything."

A few minutes later we heard the shot.

"Aren't you going to see about him?" I asked her. She didn't answer. "What are we going to do?"

"Nothing."

It seemed like a year before he shuffled up the driveway kicking dust. "Ain't nobody here cares if I live or die," he said. "Nobody even came to see about me."

Jacky stares at Mother until she looks his way and shakes

her head slightly. His penny loafers stomp across the back porch and down the wooden steps. The car door slams and his old jalopy cranks up.

"What about me?" I run out the screen door, jump on his running board and hold on to the side of his car.

"Don't worry, he won't bother you. He only hates us boys." The light from the living room window plays hopscotch on his black, Bryl-creamed hair, and his clear blue eyes are sad, but dry.

"Daddy scares the poop out of me. I never know what he's going to do."

He chuckles at my language. "I'll be back soon. I'm going out for tonight. If things get out of hand, run get Bobby. He won't let the old man hurt Mother." Our older brother lives with his family across the field on land Daddy had given him to keep him from leaving. "But try not to let Daddy scare you. Fear makes him worse."

He backs out of the driveway, and the anxiety associated with the smell of gasoline fumes set my bowels on edge. Mama always says that Jacky and I are alike, but we aren't. He is a wanderer who has been to exotic places like Miami and has even eaten pizza pie. Whatever that is. He left home for the first time when he was fourteen and I was one. But occasionally he blows in and stays a few weeks until all the molecules of air in the house begin to churn and pop because of the static. I guess Daddy resents Jacky because he is beautiful and vulnerable, but Jacky says that Mother is the one who pays. I don't know for what.

I squat to pet our big cur dog. Daddy comes to the porch to see what is going on. He has a crazed look in his eyes as he stares at the taillights of Jacky's car in the distance. "Promise me you'll never leave me," he says. "Promise."

"I promise," I say, putting my arm around his waist as far as it will go. "I'll never leave."

Right now I am violated. I feel like life is betraying me.

Daddy has threatened to kill his crazy old self, but instead he's killing me. I know it, just like I know that Jacky isn't coming back.

I run back into the house with the cur dog right behind me. I get the step stool out of the kitchen and take Pete's cage down, opening the cage door and taking him out on my finger.

"Fly, Pete!" I say. "Fly!" I hold him as high as I can and wave my hand to shoo him off.

He flaps his wings and barely clears my finger when he begins fluttering downward. "Pete's a pretty boy!" he screeches.

The cur dog sees him falling and stands with his mouth open. I try, but I can't stop what happens next. The bird's head hangs out of the dog's mouth.

Pete looks at me in desperation. "Praise the Lord! Hallelujah!" he calls to Mother.

"He did it!" she says with delight. She looks up from her crocheting just in time to see Pete swallowed whole.

I have never forgotten the piercing scream that Mother let out that night. I know now that it was that of a mother losing a child.

"I clipped his wings just yesterday! He wasn't able to fly!"

I sink to the floor, heavy with everybody's pain.

The daughter they know has died tonight and born in her place is a little girl who remembers the cage and the clipped wings. Who hates the cage and will open its door a little at a time until she can fit through and slip away for pizza pie, whatever that might be.

Hands Free
by Jill Duvall

The doors of the elevator pull open, and I step out facing a nursing station. I turn to the right and there is Mom. She stands, toothless and smiling, behind prison bars. I faint.

I wake up to the friendly male nurse holding my hand. "What happened?" I ask.

"It must of upset you to see your Mom."

No kidding, I thought. Mom is nowhere to be seen. "Can I go see her now?"

Holding onto to my arm, like I am eighty-seven instead of eighteen, he leads me back down the hall, past the elevators, and to the locked, barred wall. We enter a room at the end.

Mom is pacing back and forth between her bed and a barred window. "Hello, Mom." She looks at me and says "Hi" back, like a stranger is speaking to her. I start feeling faint again, and sit down.

"How are you feeling?" I ask, terrified to hear her answer. She is dressed in a hospital gown, brown polyester pants and house shoes. She looks frightened and her pupils are weird.

"They're trying to keep me down here, tethered to the ground."

Okay, I think, her pupils aren't just weird; she's a total freak. I turn to the nurse and ask if I can leave. Immediately.

"Sure," he says, and I wave goodbye as I jog out of that room. I shouldn't have come. I speed home in my Firebird with my mind racing, blaring my Jackson Browne eight-track as loud as I can stand it.

In the third grade, Mom had gotten sick for the first time. I rode my bike home, and Dad was strangely home at three in the afternoon instead of at work. He said Mom had to go to the hospital. She was gone for weeks. She missed my dance recital for the first time.

In the sixth grade, while I was at a sleepover, Dad had taken Mom to the hospital again.

She didn't come home for months. Granddad moved in with us, so Dad could work.

Dad had explained at dinner one night that she was very sick this time. The doctors couldn't figure out how to make it better. He asked us to pray for her.

When she had finally come home, she seemed brain dead. She didn't remember anything, including the names of the kittens born a couple of weeks before she left. Mom had named them Sonny, Cher, Festus, and Matt. My little brother had named the last one Batman, but we called him BM caused it made us laugh.

In the eighth grade, Mom left again, but was only gone a week or two. While riding down the steep side of Bradley Lane on our ten-speeds in spring that year, my best friend Donna and I saw my mother dancing on our roof.

Donna screamed over the rush of wind, "Your mom is probably insane."

"No, she's not!" I screamed back. We never talked about it again.

Up until my senior year, Mom stayed out of the hospital. Some new miracle drug had come along, and Mom had to have blood tests to keep her sane. She was still so freaky that I kept my friends away from the house.

I had no idea what mental illness was, just that Mom was strange and got sick sometimes. That all changed a week before I went to see her at the hospital.

It had been a Friday night and I had gone to a party with Donna at the house of some pot-head friend of hers. I tried to drink a beer for the first time that night, but it tasted horrible.

I poured it out on a big houseplant, and held the near-empty beer bottle for hours, feigning a deep love for beer.

Mom was at the kitchen sink when I came home. I said goodnight and kissed her cheek. I can't remember if she spoke or not.

I woke up to Mother lying on top of me, screaming, "I know you are drugs. I know it. I know it." I started screaming at her to get off and pushing back at her, but she was too strong to dislodge. Dad ran into the room and had to wrestle her off. He picked her up and carried her to the couch in the living room. I followed and watched him hold her down, while she screamed and screamed. He asked me to call the police, and I remember crying as I told them our address. The police officers were nice, but they handcuffed her. The look on her face reminded me of the look on my collie's face when he got run over by a car.

Jackson Browne is still blaring as I pull into our driveway after my troubling visit to the hospital. I am shaking and sick to my stomach. Dad and the boys aren't home, so I go to my bedroom and quickly fall into a troubled sleep.

In the dream I am two or three. Mom and I have on matching short outfits, and we are walking downtown on the sidewalk. I feel the tug on my arm reaching up to hold hands with her. She is beautiful and I keep looking at her smiling face.

Then the scene changes and Mom waves from the roof as I ride by on my bike. I pull my hands off the handlebars and ride hands-free to show off to her. She claps and I stop my ride to check on her.

Then the dream changes one last time and I am back to eighteen. Dad and I drive up to the psyche hospital in Fort Smith and in the parking lot is, nude and toothless, my mother. She crouches behind a car. I scream at Dad, "I don't want to have an insane mother. I don't want her." I open the car door to get her.

Dad wakes me up just before I reached her.

I start sobbing. "I just had the worst dream. Mom was normal and then she was sick and naked and toothless and wandering around some parking lot. It was horrible." Dad grabs my hand. "Do you think I can be normal and have a crazy mother? Or will I be like her?"

Dad waits forever before answering. "Honey, the question is not whether you'll be normal or crazy with a crazy mother. The real question is whether you will be happy or not, with a crazy mother."

That night I dream I am on my bike again, cruising down the longest hill, hands free. I seem older. Mom is there in the distance, on a roof, waving and clapping. I wave back but, this time, I keep racing on by.

Do You Remember Me?

by Jay Freidrich

It was Sunday, July 31, 1949, when the boat carrying my dad and Mr. Hubert Beck and his three children rounded the point on a small lake and disappeared out of sight. Danny Beck, the youngest of the Beck children, was two years old that day. Danny's birthday and the hot, humid Sunday afternoon were good reasons for all of us to spend an afternoon picnicking, swimming, and boating.

Our family—my mom and dad, my three sisters, my brother and I—were enjoying a summer outing with several aunts and uncles and with another family of friends from our parish—Hubert Beck, his wife, and their three children. At nine, I was the oldest of the eight children there, and we were all taking turns riding in the boat. Danny and my sister Sue, who was almost three, hadn't been allowed to ride in the boat because their mothers thought they were too young. That didn't seem to bother Sue, but Danny cried to go along every time the boat left.

His daddy was in it. Finally, Danny's mother relented, and the boat took off with my dad, Mr. Beck, and the three Beck children aboard. In just a couple of minutes, they rounded the point and were out of sight.

It was a while before anyone realized that the boat hadn't returned. Then someone noticed swimmers leaving the swimming area and swimming across the lake toward the area where the boat had last been seen. One of my uncles commented that it was dangerous for swimmers to swim in the boating area. Soon it was obvious that something was wrong because more swimmers were crossing the lake.

Somehow, we learned later, the boat had capsized. According to Mr. Beck, my dad grabbed the two Beck girls and swam to the shore about fifty feet away. Mr. Beck, who was not a strong swimmer, tried to make it to the shore with Danny, but Danny slipped out of his grip and disappeared beneath the water. As he struggled ashore to care for his girls, Mr. Beck saw my dad returning for Danny. Then he saw Dad disappear too.

Standing on the shore with his two daughters, Mr. Beck directed the first swimmers on the scene to the spot where he had seen Danny and my dad disappear. In less than fifteen minutes they had my dad on shore, but they could not resuscitate him. They didn't find Danny until the next morning.

* * *

Christmas Eve in 1949 was our first Christmas without our dad. It was also the first Christmas that Santa Claus visited our home. After supper on Christmas Eve, Mom and my aunt and uncle took us to our grandfather's farm out in the country, just as Mom and Dad had always done. Like he had every Christmas I could remember, Grandpa gave the five of us each a silver dollar. We visited a while and then returned home to see that, just like in Christmases past, while we were away, gifts had appeared under the Christmas tree in our living room. But before we could begin opening our gifts, which we had always done on Christmas Eve in the past, there was the sound of bells and a knock on the front door. My uncle went to the door, opened it, and in walked Santa with a big bag of packages.

Santa sat down, called each of us by name, asked whether we had been good, then had the five of us line up along the wall across the room from him. "Can you say your prayers for me?" he asked. First me, then my sister Carolyn, and finally my sister Betty—each of us recited a prayer for him. Phil and Sue were still too young to pray alone. Then he asked us all to sing for him. Singing was something we loved to do, so we sang several Christmas songs for him. Finally he opened his bag and began distributing gifts to us. After a little more chitchat with us and the adults he said he needed to be on his way and left.

He came again the next year, and the next, and for several more years after that. Every year the routine was the same: call us each by name, ask us to say our prayers for him, and listen as we sang as a group for him. I don't remember whether it was that first year or the next year that I asked my sister Carolyn, who was only a year younger than me, whether she knew who Santa was. He had to be someone we knew because of some of the things he said each year, but I couldn't figure out whom. Neither could Carolyn. After Santa's Christmas visit each of the next several years Carolyn and I would discuss who Santa might be. We never could figure it out, and eventually we quit trying.

* * *

On October 3, 1994, Mother died after a five-year bout with liver cancer. She had raised her five children alone, working at two jobs for almost forty years to support herself and her children and to see each of them through twelve years of Catholic schools and into college.

I was living in Indiana then and had traveled to Little Rock to see her in the hospital and say goodbye two days before she died. My wife, Cecelia, our children and I returned to Little Rock for the Vigil Service and funeral, arriving just a couple of hours before the Vigil Service began with Mother's favorite prayer—the Rosary.

After the Rosary many people came up to offer their

condolences, as people always do. Many of them I recognized immediately. Some I barely knew. I had left Little Rock more than thirty years earlier, returning only for visits with family and a few close friends. Consequently, many of my encounters, particularly with the older visitors, began with them asking, "Do you remember me?" Sometimes that was followed with "I worked with your mother," or "I was your mother's postman," or "I belonged to St. Edward's with your mother," or "I was your mother's neighbor." Sometimes I would remember them and sometimes I wouldn't, but as we always are at times like this, I was impressed by the many people my mother's life had touched.

Then, suddenly, an elderly man was there, my sister Carolyn by his side. "Do you remember me?" he said. I looked, but had to say, "No, I'm sorry. I don't." I looked at Carolyn. She didn't say a word, but I saw the beginning of a smile shining in her eyes.

"You used to pray for me, and you used to sing for me," he said. And after a brief pause, he continued, "I'm Santa Claus."

"Jay," Carolyn said, "This is Hubert Beck."

I laughed and said hello, and then, before I had a chance to think, I felt tears trickling down my cheeks.

Seasons

by Kevin Brockmeier

I. July, Little Rock, 1983

There are things no one tells you about the summer.

When you are ten years old, finally grown-up enough to stay home without a babysitter, and you have spent the morning pressing your tape recorder to the TV to capture your favorite theme songs, no one tells you that you are not wasting your day.

No one tells you that a summer day, in June, in 1983, cannot be wasted.

Jeff, who is your younger brother, begins repeating, "Shhh, be quiet, Jeff! Jeff, I said be quiet!" during the opening credits of *Welcome Back, Kotter*, and you yell at him for ruining the recording. No one tells you if your dreams are your ticket out, and years later, when you replay the tape, you will be astonished by your voice and its pipsqueak venom.

It is nearly one o'clock by the time Scott Hayden, your best friend, arrives at your back door. He has already eaten lunch, and so have you, as well as your post-lunch snack. Jeff is upstairs pedaling your mom's antique sewing machine, whose wheel you can hear thrumming like a train through the floor, and you and Scott seize the chance to sneak outside without him. The air is so damp and sticky that everything you say seems to emerge in its own heavy syrup, like sap from a tree, each sentence falling splat against the pavement. As a rule, the weather in Little Rock has this effect on people until mid-September, when the first cool rains arrive and all the old conversations dissolve and wash away.

You walk to Star Systems, the video arcade, which is two blocks from Sturbridge, the apartment complex where you both live. Scott keeps threatening to moon the cars on Rodney Parham, and he might actually do it. He is crazy, hilarious, in the best and most exasperating way, so electric-wiry and fickle that every hour you spend with him becomes a beautiful, needless adventure. He likes to embarrass you at the drugstore by drooling onto the floor or by pretending, loudly, that he has caught you stealing candy. Once, as a prank, he douses his shoes in insect repellent, sets them alight, and strolls through the self-service bay of an Exxon station. No one tells you what will happen to him one day.

The token machine at Star Systems is out of order, which means that you have to exchange your money at the counter. You have seventy-five cents, which you are carrying in your shoe because your shorts have no pockets. Slowly you peel the coins from the sole of your foot, handing them one by one to the girl at the counter, who wrinkles her nose and pinches them between her fingernails. No one tells you what she might be thinking. Your favorite game is *Q*Bert*, because of the little orange hero with the flat feet and the gun-barrel nose, but you have never mastered the game's peculiar slanting style of play, and before you know it, your lives have drained away—every one of them. You watch Scott steer through the Pole Position course, the same billboards and white clouds drifting by again and again until he crashes for the last time, and then you return to his apartment, where the two of you drink Shastas and eat Fruit Roll- Ups.

"Do you want to see something cool?" he asks, and shows you the big bag of fireworks his dad has bought for the Fourth of July: bottle rockets, firecrackers, even a handful of M-80s— illegal, but there they are anyway. "Dad keeps the lighter with him in the car," Scott says. "At all times. But that won't be a problem if you'll help me out, man." You follow him to Bruno's Little Italy, which is separated from the apartments by a pair of parking lots, their tar-baked gray by the heat. Scott spins a story about his missing dog for the restaurant's hostess—half-Irish Setter and half-Golden Retriever, a puppy, in fact, a puppy named Patsy, Patsy O'Malley, who went running this way not three minutes ago, has anyone seen her, oh where could she possibly be—while you snatch a couple of matchbooks from the basket in the foyer. Then together you head for the creek.

You take turns firing bottle rockets into the water, watching the white bubbles that wobble to the surface and belch their smoke into the air. No one tells you how many fish you might be killing. The M-80s are powerful, but when you bury them in the clay of the creek bed, they explode only down to the waist, creating smooth open moon craters with red cardboard cylinders in the center. The firecrackers, on the other hand, burst with a satisfying spray of yellow muck, leaving behind a maze of smoking caverns, and it is easy to imagine a smaller version of yourself exploring them.

Scott leads you back to the courtyard. On a dare, you shoot a few bottle rockets onto the tall, sloping roof of the apartment where Rodney lives—Rodney, who is sixteen, drinks beer, and rides a motorcycle; Rodney, who on Friday and Saturday nights escorts his girlfriends into the woods behind the apartment complex, where he has stashed a shabby mattress that you and Scott keep booby-trapping with pine cones. The bottle rockets go zinging up the roof's ramp of shingles, detonating at the ridgeline or in midair. You manage to fire off half a dozen before Rodney comes bounding outside to chase you. He is not wearing his shoes, and by climbing through the pile of rocks behind the dumpster, the two of you are easily able to escape him. From a distance, you taunt him, and he curses back at you with words that are worse than any you have ever heard, a mother without the f, a god without the d, using two- and three-syllable substitutions that glint with a strange dirty mystery. No one tells you what will happen to

Rodney one day, either.

The rest of the afternoon you spend riding your bikes and unearthing balls from the scrub behind the tennis courts and dissecting the pods you find growing on a plant by the mailboxes, peeling the rinds from around the moist brain-like nuts and smelling the tang they leave on your skin. It is past rush hour by the time you return home. Scott's dad is angry with him for stealing the family's fireworks, and your mom is angry with you for leaving your brother unsupervised. There they stand, together in the courtyard, saying, "You're in trouble, Mister. The both of you. Big, big trouble," but it doesn't matter, it doesn't matter at all, because this is not their summer, it is yours, it belongs to you, it will never belong to you so completely again, which is something else no one ever tells you about the summer.

II. Three and a Half Snows

1.

I was four years old before I saw my first snowfall. It happened just after my family moved from Coral Springs, Florida, to Little Rock, Arkansas. I woke one morning to an unusual vacancy of sound. The silence seemed to swell against itself like the silence inside a tunnel, and immediately I knew that something was different. My bedroom was partially submerged below the front yard, the high window level with the grass. I poured myself a bowl of cereal, pulled a chair up to the wall, and stood looking out at the transformed neighborhood: at the still white river of the street, the smoothly flowing hills where the rocks used to be, the oak trees etched down to the smallest twig. It all had the quality of a secret.

2.

Some five years later, during the largest snowfall of my

childhood, I was playing in the field alongside my house when a camera operator came trudging through the banks. "Hey, kid! Do something interesting!" he shouted. I was not a coordinated person—whenever I threw a Frisbee, it would peel off to the side, rolling away from me like a hubcap—but I packed a snowball, cocked my arm, and hit the lens of his camera from a distance of forty feet. I was afraid I had broken something and ran away. That night, my mom called me into the living room to show me the teaser that kept playing on the local news. For a long time after, every time it snowed in Little Rock, I would see myself on television, making the one and only miracle throw of my life.

3.

Once, when I was in the fifth grade, it began to snow so hard and unexpectedly that the second half of the school day was cancelled. Our parents were called to pick us up. The classroom slowly emptied out as we watched the air beyond the window swirl in a lazy net. Eventually only two of us were left—me and Stacey Bell, a girl I had been in love with for five years and would remain in love with for another four, until I transferred to a different high school. Our teacher locked the room and took us to the foyer. The air was so cold I could see my breath mingling with Stacey's against the broad glass doors. It was a moment of dreamlike intimacy. There seemed the possibility, however remote, that she would kiss me. The world was a marvelous place.

½.

Though my life has sometimes carried me away from Little Rock, I have always returned. I know the city well. The seasons here have taken on a different texture recently, the winters becoming more temperate and the summers becoming less. Most years offer no more than a day or two of freezing weather, with just enough snowfall for me to press my footprints into the pavement for a few seconds before they turn to water. Sometimes, in the momentary dusting that comes down on a February afternoon, I remember the way my street looked through the high window of my bedroom when everything was cocooned in white. It hasn't snowed like that here in years.

III. Last Words

My grandfather said, "Okay, I'm ready to go home."

He said, "Can you work the lock? I can't reach it from the inside."

He said, "How does something like this happen? Why won't the damn thing open?"

The night before, he had climbed over the side rail of his bed, falling and bruising his hip, and the hospital's head nurse had instructed that a protective net be fastened to the frame to prevent him from doing so again. The net was suspended over the bed on four posts, shoeboxing him inside. He was ninety-eight. His heart was failing. The doctor had made it plain to us that any word he uttered could be his last. Maybe that was why every sentence he spoke seemed to cap itself off as I listened, passing over into an enigmatic final pronouncement.

He said, "I never imagined I would end up trapped in here."

He said, "If only someone had told me when I was a child."

He said, "This is completely ridiculous."

My mother had taken her cell phone into the hall to check her messages, and for the moment I was alone with him. I didn't know what to say. The net around his bed was zipped shut, but it would have been a simple thing for me to open it. If I did, though, I knew he would begin asking for his shoes again, trying to sit up and insisting that I drive him home. And perhaps that would be the right thing to do, I thought, to drive him home, but the decision had not been left to me.

In 1997, a few months apart and at the urging of my

mother, we had both moved to Little Rock, Arkansas. I was returning from graduate school, hoping to figure out a way to meet the rest of my life, and he was relocating from his apartment in Miami, hoping, I imagined, for the same. We all believed he would live for another year or two, but instead he lasted for nearly a decade.

At first, the impression I carried of him was left over from my childhood: he was my short, fat grandpa, as opposed to my tall, thin one. Once or twice a year he would visit from Florida, preparing elaborate Italian dishes from scratch, playing Banker-Broker with my brother and me, and singing "Ah, Sweet Mystery of Life" as he walked through our house. Gradually, though, sitting over the dinner table or helping him pick his way through the grocery store, I came to know him better. He was born in 1907 into a home that was later demolished to make way for the World Trade Center. He left school at fourteen to become a butcher, a trade that paid well enough for him to assist his entire family through the Great Depression and still buy a new car every year. He married late and fathered two children, the first before shipping out for WWII and the second after he was discharged. His wife died of breast cancer a few years before I was born.

Shortly after he moved into the retirement center, the rare single man among a multitude of single women, he was approached several times by neighbors angling to strike up a romance with him. To them, he answered, "That phase of my life is over." To me, he explained, "What do I want with a bunch of old bags?"

In 2001, I took him to see the movie *Malena*. He knew he was going to die soon, he said, and he wanted to brush up on his Italian so that he would be able to converse with his relatives when he saw them in Heaven. The movie had its share of sex and profanity, and I wondered if he would be offended by it, but afterward his only complaint was with the fact that the Italian spoken by the characters was not his native dialect.

Now here he was in the hospital saying, "If we could just find a way to undo the lock, Kevin, you could get me out of here."

I said, "I'm sorry. I can't open it for you."

I said, "The doctors want you to stay in bed, Grandpa. I'm not supposed to let you out."

I said, "Nobody here wants you to hurt yourself."

For a moment he was confused. Then he was furious. In a flare of energy, he made two fists, punching the mattress on either side of his body.

He said, "I guess you're not as good a person as I thought you were."

Not long after, I went home to get some sleep. When I returned the next afternoon, my grandfather had taken on a surprising placidity. The net had been removed from his bed, and he lay staring at the ceiling, working his lips over his gums. Toward evening he noticed my mother standing beside him. He extended his hand. He said, "Well, I'm dying now. It was a pleasure to know you."

Were these his last words? It depends on your perspective. He lived for another week, but by the next morning, he had already free-fallen into his past, beginning that slow dive of the mind that would carry him back through his retirement, his marriage, his youth, and his childhood to the silence of his final sleep. Though they were not the last words to leave his mouth, they were the last words spoken by the man I had come to know, or at least by the person I thought he was.

For Love and Travel

by Frank Thurmond

When my friend Brad found me at a table in the Gloucester Arms pub in Oxford, England, I was studying a shamrock drawn upon the creamy top of a cool thick pint of dark stout. The late afternoon sun had finally impaled the English clouds, revealing wisps of blue sky after a dull grey morning of cold drizzle. Brad sat down across from me.

"You okay?"

As I looked up I realized too late my face was streaked with tears, and my friend was taken aback. We'd known each other several years now, fellow "Yanks" at Oxford who'd connected as being both from the South—with all its associated idiosyncrasies that few other compatriots seemed to appreciate.

"I just heard from my father . . . " I hardly spoke the words before I found it difficult to go on. "I think I told you once that I never knew him."

Brad nodded thoughtfully. "Yes, I remember your mentioning that."

"Not since I was three years old at least, when he left." I paused again to regain composure as Brad waited. As I struggled to express my predicament, I felt a profound sense of gratitude simply for having a friend there to listen. I drank a deep sip of beer, savoring its cool, bitter taste as someone put a song on the jukebox behind us and a heavy rock ballad started to play. I took a deep breath and continued.

"My mother called to say she'd heard from him. Or from his family, rather. They said my father's on his deathbed dying of lung cancer. The doctor says he's got less than a week to live, and now he wants to speak with me before he dies."

Brad's reply threw me for a loop. "You have to go see him," he said.

"What?"

"You should get on the next flight home to the States and meet your father before he dies. You'll always regret it if you don't." He was speaking from experience, having lost his own father prematurely.

The only way I could ever confront the lifelong sense of emptiness I had endured was to finally meet, just once before he died, the father I had never known. This was the only way I might achieve a true sense of closure. By the end of the evening I had made my decision. I would travel home to meet my father.

My old school friend Robert offered to travel with me from Little Rock to Hot Springs so I wouldn't have to journey there alone. We drove up the day before my appointment with my father and stayed the night in a hotel on Lake Hamilton. Then the next day we drove to the house where my father had lived with his girlfriend and her family for many years. I was greeted in the front yard by a man of about my own age named Randall.

"I know exactly what you're experiencing," he said. "I met my own birth father later in life too." By the time we entered the house, Randall explained how he was brought up in turn by my biological father like a son of his own. (My father had otherwise had no further children.) I was still processing this when I was greeted at the door by Randall's mother, Monica. She welcomed me graciously and led me into the living room, where several other women—including Randall's wife and sister—waited.

"He's in the back room," said Monica. "He's expecting you." Robert waited with Randall as I followed Monica into the back of the house. We entered the back room, and there he was, sitting in a chair waiting for me. Randall had quickly explained that the only reason my father wasn't in a hospital bed hooked up to a ventilator was that he'd wanted to meet me with dignity. So they'd had the machine set up here, next to his chair.

Monica showed me to a seat and then discreetly left the room. I didn't know what to say, but I knew an attempt at small talk would seem, under the circumstances, pathetic. But he spoke first.

He said: "You're studying English literature?" I could tell from his voice that his health had already declined rapidly since our brief phone conversation three days earlier.

"Yes, I'm studying medieval and Renaissance drama."

Then to my surprise he began to recite Chaucer in Middle English:

"Whan that April with his showres soote The droughte of March hath perced to the roote . . . "

I suddenly realized the room we were in was a private study full of books. There were books everywhere, with every imaginable title from Dostoevsky to Chomsky to a treatise on the art of growing marijuana.

He told me of his archaeological research in England, and showed me photographs from his travels. He then commended me for my academic success, and said he'd been pleased to hear it.

I said: "I guess you gave me some good genes."

"You got your genes from your mother." Suddenly he began coughing violently, and Monica rushed into the room to adjust the ventilator. It was clear that our conversation was becoming extremely difficult for him. I looked into his eyes and was struck by a strange sense of familiarity, and then realized his eyes seemed the mirror image of my own. Yet they now betrayed something else, too—something he would finally express before we said goodbye.

It seemed an appropriate moment for bringing the visit to a

close. I told my father simply how glad I was finally to have met him. I told him that I would one day write about our meeting, so that this occasion (and he) would not be forgotten. It was now my turn to quote poetry, and I recalled two lines which seemed to fit the sentiment perfectly:

"So long as men can breathe, or eyes can see,/So long lives this, and this gives life to thee."

My father nodded. Then I said: "I want you to know that as you are my father, I love you."

Just as I was about to leave, he seemed to be struggling to summon up one last word.

"Don't die bitter," he said. Then he looked deeply into my eyes before saying the last words I would ever hear from him: "I regret." With this he abruptly dropped his chin to his chest with a look of final resignation.

As I turned away my eyes filled with tears, and when they saw my face the women in the room began to weep. Randall accompanied me outside where Robert was waiting at the car, and I thanked him for helping make my visit such a warm one. Then Monica came out and said she had something for me from my father.

"He insisted on this," she said, handing me a check to cover the cost of my trip from London. On the check he had written: "For love and travel."

The next day, Randall called to say my father had died that night. He had left me all his books. "He spent the last few days of his life trying to tie up all the loose ends before you arrived," Randall explained. "We told him he should just rest and save energy, and that we'd take care of everything. Yet he insisted, and just kept saying—but I have promises to keep."

I smiled, and then recited softly to myself: And miles to go before I sleep.

Mermaids, Jellyfish, and Oncoming Traffic: The Summer of 1984

by Phillip Taylor

I really don't remember much about the 1984 World's Fair in New Orleans except for the enormous topless mermaids gracing the entranceway as I stood in line with my dad and eight more of my sweating family members. But for a nine-year-old boy, I guess that is all you really need.

It was the first leg of our family road trip that summer that started out with my immediate family leaving Malvern, Arkansas in the middle of the night to meet up with other family members in Pine Bluff. There were ten of us altogether: my evangelist father, my mother, and my six-year-old brother Brandon; my aunt and stick-in-the mud uncle (by marriage); my denim cut-off jean-shorts wearing uncle and his seven-year-old daughter; my grandmother, and my mom's youngest sister. We all crammed into two cars: a maroon station wagon with gold and white stripes and a light blue Ford LTD.

Luckily, for our safety and well-being, short shorts, mesh tank tops, and half-shirts were popular back then. What today would certainly be really bad fashion was actually a lifesaver in the sticky summer of New Orleans as we filed into the World's Fair.

The image of the mermaids stayed with me long after driving out of New Orleans. I remember little else until we stood on the beach in Biloxi, Mississippi. The disgustingly brown Gulf of Mexico waves hardly lapped, and I think there was even a bit of a stench. Seeing as how not many people were swimming in the Gulf, the adults decided we'd take a boat ride out to Ship Island, an incredible island that was an old fort during the nineteenth century.

As our boat to Ship Island took us further and further from the Mississippi coast we became surrounded by beautiful, pristine water, as if we were taking a ferry out of a fecal bath and landing in the Caribbean. We docked, set up on the soft, white sand, and jumped in the water. I did notice that the adults were freaking out over these ugly, transparent landmines they called jellyfish that littered the luscious shoreline, but I had no time for such worries. Then, when we were nearly finished with our fabulous swimming excursion, my brother Brandon took a full-blown hit to the torso. You would have thought it was the end of the world. Family members thrashed through the water. Adults screamed. Children cried. People gathered to witness the carnage. The horror! Oh, the horror! The absolute terror of what turned out to be a small child being grazed by a jellyfish.

The Jellyfish Massacre took a close second to the Topless Mermaids, and we moved on eastward.

Next stop was Mobile, Alabama and the *U.S.S. Alabama* battleship. Now, I am a little fuzzy on the details of what exactly happened next. Maybe it was the distraction of the squelch from the CB or maybe it was the sheer splendor that is known as Mobile, Alabama, but whatever it was, it distracted my father. We were separated from the other car in our caravan. My father knew we were supposed to go through a tunnel to get to the battleship, so we were all relieved when we saw the curve leading into the tunnel. Resting assured that we were on the right track, I noticed the brilliant lights of the tunnel that was about to engulf us in its illumination. Then, I noticed the headlights.

As we were nearly through the curve leading into the tunnel—in the wrong direction—my uncle shouted, which jarred my father out of his trance, thus causing him to swerve into the correct lane and avoid a head-on collision. We sat in silence as my Uncle Denim's swear—a word that sounds very similar to what were on our way to see—echoed throughout the cavernous station wagon.

Topless Mermaids, a Jellyfish Massacre, and now the Tunnel of Death. What could possibly be next? It didn't take long to find out.

After the *U.S.S. Alabama*, we headed to our final destination, Pensacola, Florida. My Uncle Stick-in-the-Mud was a bit of what most people would consider to be a jerk. My dad had gone snorkeling on the other side of the sparkling white sand dunes with my Uncle Denim whilst my brother and I chased seagulls and picked up shells. After I had not seen my dad for a while, I became alarmed that something bad might have happened. I panicked. I found Uncle Stick-in-the-Mud, who matter-of-factly told me that my dad was stung by an electric eel and had died. What? Surely I heard him wrong, so I asked again.

"Yep, he was killed my an electric eel," repeated Uncle Stick-in-the-Mud, as he laughed.

Having witnessed the sheer devastation of a jellyfish sting just a few days prior, I could only imagine stumbling upon the charred remains of my father. I ran around the beach with tears flowing from my face while the wind spackled the powdery sand onto my boney cheeks. Instead of concealing my emotions, the mixture of tears, sand, and snot gave me the appearance of a tusked creature grieving for the loss of its father.

I then saw my father emerge atop a sand dune, un-charred and very much alive. I ran to him and wrapped my frail, lanky frame around his legs. I could not have been happier to see him. Slobber, sand, and pure emotion stuck to the limbs of the man that had stood with me in the shadow of giant, topless mermaids, splashed through the Gulf to save my brother from certain jellyfish slaughter, and nearly driven me to my death a few days earlier, but for me, it was a very magical moment in the summer of 1984. And though I didn't know if then, it would be one of several I would never forget.

A Day at the Snake House

by Velda Brotherton

We circled through the yard, past a small flower garden lush with lilies and iris. Up a steep incline we climbed toward a compact cinder block building shoved into the rocks above the house. Fred unlocked the door and pulled it open. An odor wafted from the dark interior. Something feral and warm, not unpleasant, just unusual. Hair on my neck wavered, my sixth sense prickled. He stepped into the snake house, and I followed. Brave to the end.

Just three days earlier I had mustered up the courage (or ignorance) to call Fred Lally, AKA The Snake Man. It was 1990 and I was a feature writer for the weekly *Washington County Observer* in rural northwest Arkansas. Any trip to town took me by his large trailer painted with all manner of reptiles and snuggled into a pocket in the bluffs that lined the east side of the highway. Though mortified by the very thought of a snake, it was inevitable that one day I would ask him for an interview. Who could pass it up? As far as I knew no one else had ever written about him. It wasn't long before I figured out why.

When I called he was quiet for a while, then said in his soft voice, "You'll want to see my snakes." It wasn't a question.

Living in the wilderness of the Ozarks, I've occasionally experienced face-to-face encounters with the evil little crawlers. It's an understatement to say we have plenty of snakes in these hills. All four of the continent's poisonous snakes live somewhere in Arkansas, three of them in our part of the state. The best thing is, we rarely see them, but we know they're around. Lurking under rocks and boards and fallen trees.

So when Fred Lally made it fairly clear that it would be "interview me, interview my snakes," I had to reach a quick decision. Did I want to chicken out or go for it? I'm thinking here, small snakes, and definitely not poisonous ones. They'd be in boxes or cages or terrariums, surely. Yes, I could do it.

With a quiver in my voice, I answered, "Of course I want to see your snakes."

"Okay, come on up to the house around nine, and we'll talk, I'll arrange for a visit with the big guys."

I managed to croak, "Big guys?"

Calm as could be he said, "Got me one of the longest reticulated pythons in captivity."

I had no idea what a reticulated python was or how big it might be. In too deep to back out, I said, "Okay, I look forward to visiting with the big guys."

When Tuesday rolled around I was so scared I could barely climb out of my car at the Snake Man's house. But I put on one heck of a front. If nothing else, I was determined Fred wouldn't see the tentacles of fear slithering through me. He was, after all, an expert in his field. Surely he wouldn't stand by while one of his creatures buried its fangs deep in my skin. Or one of the big guys swallowed me whole.

A small-framed wiry man whose age could've been thirty or fifty answered my timid knock. He didn't appear the sort who could wrestle with twenty- to thirty-foot pythons.

We were no more than inside till he held up his deformed right hand.

"See that?" He wiggled the remaining digits. Two fingers were all the way gone, another part of the way. A shudder worked its way through me.

"Rattlesnake bit me and it got infected. Lost my fingers." At this point, praying was all I could manage. "Another time, I made a big mistake when I went to feed the pythons. See, I feed 'em whole raw chickens and I forgot to wash really good after handling the chickens. When I stepped in with him, he got a whiff and was right on me. Opened his mouth wide and closed it around my head." He actually chuckled again. "Thought I was supper, don't you see?"

He eyed me a moment, eyes flashing, and went on. He was getting one heck of a kick out of scaring me witless. With that realization came another. What if this was part of his act? He'd said they had a show in Florida. This could be an example of what he did. He went right on with his gory tale.

"Took three men to pry him loose and I about suffocated before they did. You gotta be careful around these snakes. Some of 'em can kill you with a bite, others can squeeze you to death, others are tame as kittens and couldn't hurt you if they wanted to. Course, a non-venomous bite can get infected . . ." He held up the hand, "and there you go."

I caught that look again. Yes, while he might be telling the truth, this man was having a ball putting fear into me. He needn't have worried. I'd come equipped with that. The danger to me if—no, when—I followed him into his snake house was probably nil. He just wanted to scare me half to death because it was his way of having fun.

Pen poised, I asked as brightly as I could manage, "So, how did you get started, uh," gulp, "doing this?"

To his credit, he settled down to business and we spent the next thirty minutes or so, me asking, him answering what I hoped were intelligent questions. Finally, when I could think of no more, and believe me I tried, he determined it was time we went to the snake house so he could introduce me around.

"Let's go see the big guys first, then," he said.

I stepped into the dark snake house after Fred and the door quietly shut behind me. I couldn't see anything yet because my eyes hadn't adjusted to the dark. And that's when I heard something. Fred hadn't spoken and neither had I, so what was that sound? I held my breath and listened some more. Sighing . . . no, too measured.

I could hear them breathing! I couldn't see them yet, but I could smell them and hear them. Yes. Fred stepped to one side. By then I could make out their shapes in the dim light.

Great coils piled on wooden beds built along the walls. And that's when I realized there were no cages to hold them. I was truly in their midst. A desire crept through me. A great need to touch them, to commune. I glanced at Fred, then took a step and reached out.

"Go ahead," he said softly. "They like to be touched."

As if out of my control, my hand lifted toward the shadowy mass, patted, then firmly caressed the palpating coil of a live reticulated python. Bigger around than my own body, and I'm no lightweight, it's great length lay twined in and out, round and round. Cool to the touch, the musculature rose and fell under my palm.

Fred's story of his head being swallowed echoed in my head. Amid all the coils, no mouth was visible.

"Tell you what," Fred said over my shoulder. "Let's take one outside in the sunlight where you can get a good look at him. What do you say?"

I didn't move. What if it escaped, took off for the woods? Imagine some hunter coming across this hefty fellow.

He must've recognized my hesitation, because he said, "Don't worry, they've all been fed. They won't eat again for weeks."

My laugh joined his, and enthusiasm overcame the last of my reluctance.

"Maybe you'd like to hold one?"

I would, yes, indeed I would.

This brave, foolish woman couldn't be me.

Then he accomplished the most amazing feat. He dug into the massive coils—at that point, it was impossible to tell how many were there—and began to work that tremendous body loose from the others.

It appeared to cooperate and together they moved—one

walking the other slithering—out of the snake house and into the grassy sunlight.

Fred's wife Carol was waiting outside and knelt down in the grass. She maneuvered the great head by placing one open hand under the throat, sat down and draped a few coils around on her lap. The remainder of its length spread out across the yard. After taking a few pictures, I lay down the camera and Carol carefully transferred the coils to my lap. The python's huge golden eyes studied me closely and its muscles flexed gently over my legs and arms. Our gazes connected. For the flick of an instant I existed in a distant past where man's footprints had not yet been set into the soil of this earth.

Scarcely moving, he lolled under MY touch, only lifting his head to regard ME. Eye to eye.

"He's magnificent," I murmured, and wished there were other words in our language to express how I felt.

"What is reticulated?" I asked, gently rubbing the bright brown and black diamond patches drawn on his body, as if I'd always known how to do this. Braver, I showed off a little, closely studying his huge mouth.

Thankfully, it remained shut tight all the while. I don't know what I'd have done if he'd yawned.

"He gets the name because of the way he's marked," Fred explained. "Reticulated means having lines intercrossed, forming a network. He's also known as a regal python which means king."

I grinned. "Hard to write all that down while I'm holding him."

"We'll go over it again," he promised. "Before you leave I've got some others to show you."

I gulped and my lap buddy clenched, raised his tremendous head above mine and wavered around a bit. I felt my stomach instantly knot as primal fear clamped down on me like a vise. To this day I believe it sensed my moment of trepidation.

Fred quickly stepped in and guided the enormous snake

from me to him and back toward his domain with little trouble. The regal monarch's dark brown skin shone in the sunlight. I watched the last of his graceful body slither into the darkness of his realm, and a part of my psyche awakened from a deep sleep. I had connected with an incredible species in a way that few people ever do, and learned a valuable lesson about respecting God's creatures.

The door to the snake house closed, and I wondered if that python would remember me the way I knew I would never forget him.

Rosco the Devil Chicken

by Stan Whisman

Take Rosco home to perk up your hens," Grandpa said as he loaded the coop with the young rooster into our trunk. I thought I saw Rosco glare at me as the lid was closed. Maybe just my imagination.

My grandpa was a strange fellow. He lived alone in a one-room cabin in the woods until he was ninety-two years old, then finally took ill and moved to a nursing facility, maybe the first time he had enjoyed running water. But that was not what made him so strange. It was his other habits that make me say that. Grandpa liked tinkering with animal husbandry and such. He was always trying to cross a dog with a coyote, and a chicken with a pheasant. He thought someday he would be famous for his crossbred mutant animals. He did once have an article written about him in a state newspaper, which only served to encourage him to try harder. I remember our annual trips to his cabin when he would take us on a tour of the homestead and show off his creatures. "This one is five-eights chicken and three-eights pheasant," he would announce as we passed a coop with a strange looking bird strutting around the back.

Grandpa waved as we pulled out of the drive onto the dirt road, dust rolling up behind the car.

The two-hour trip home was boring as usual and as we drove up to our house and opened the trunk Rosco began to crow and announce his presence immediately to our flock of Barred Rocks and Rhode Island Reds. The bigger and older roosters rushed over to check out this new kid on the block.

Rosco didn't take too kindly to this show of affection and immediately started shucking feathers off of the largest of our roosters. Rosco was less than half his size, but it only took him a minute or two to totally humble and humiliate the large red. The big fellow would make a swat towards Rosco and the little guy would jump in his face and claw crazily until the red had had enough and turned to run. Big Red thought it was all over, but it was only the beginning. The faster he ran, the more Rosco was on him from the rear and I felt his pain as I saw them disappearing over the horizon with Red's feathers flying up into the sky as far as I could see. I thought it was funny to see the small rooster making such a mess of Big Red's day, but little did I know that Rosco was looking forward to teaching me a lesson as well.

The very next day as I strolled leisurely out the door to go swimming in the pond, Rosco came boldly from the chicken yard and stood in front of me with a daring look in his eyes. My first thought was, "Look at this silly little chicken thinking he's going to fight me!" I picked up a stick, thinking I'd get this off his mind as soon as possible. Rosco made a run at my naked legs and I swung the stick. I hit nothing but air.

Rosco nailed me in the shin and backed away to gather for another blow. I rubbed my shin and drew back the stick again for another try as he rushed in—shwish—nothing but air again as Rosco plowed into my other shin with his wings and spurs.

I don't mind telling you that I felt a little overwhelmed at about that point, and decided to save the rest of the battle for another day as I turned and ran towards the barn with the little devil right on my heels. I hit the hayloft ladder and took the steps two at a time as Rosco backed off and paced back and forth strutting proudly. I finally slipped out the other side of the barn when Rosco wasn't looking and made it back to the safety of the house.

Over the next few days, Rosco pretty much kept me at bay in the house. Mom was wondering why I wasn't playing outside these days. I was ashamed to admit that I was bettered by a little chicken, so I told her I didn't feel good, which worked until she started threatening me with an enema if I didn't get better (that was Mom's cure for everything). I knew I had to either face Rosco or face the enema bag.

I started sneaking out the back door of the house and peeking around each corner to keep away from Rosco. Every time he saw me, he'd make another pass at me until I went up a tree or got back into the safety of the house or barn. I laid awake at night trying to figure a way to get out of this situation that had made such a wreck of my summer days, until I mastered a plan. I finally realized why man is at the top of the food chain. It was a new game.

I awoke the next morning full of hope and anxious to execute my plan. I whistled softly as I strode out the back door towards the barn. As if on cue, Rosco came alert at my appearance and launched at a run to whop my legs as usual. I set sail for the barn and hit the loft ladder just inches ahead of the foul fowl flying up to the loft as Rosco strutted about at the base of the ladder quite enjoying his moment of victory. Knowing dad would need a bale of hay to feed the milk cow when he got home, I picked that very moment to throw down a full bale of hay to lessen dad's chores. It was with sadness that I strolled back to the house and reported the accident to Mom.

Mom had a way with fried chicken, and we were a little on the poor side, not bad enough to search for road kill, but bad enough to not waste food, either. I ate wildly at supper that evening, that chicken all golden-brown with mashed potatoes and gravy along the side. And as I took my last bite of that scrumptious drumstick, I told Mom that was the best fried chicken I'd ever had. Then, with a nod and a wink, I looked straight at Mom and said, "Save that wishbone for me!"

The Last Days of Ray Winder Field
by Jay Jennings

On a muggy Thursday night in July of 2006, program in hand, I took a seat in the bleachers behind home plate at Little Rock's Ray Winder Field, home of the Arkansas Travelers, a Double-A minor-league baseball team. The Wurlitzer was pumping out the chestnut "Here We Go, Travelers, Here We Go [Clap, Clap]." The program was filled with badly designed ads for local businesses like pawn shops and towing companies and featured several "Lucky Number" pages with figures in red to be matched with those announced between innings over the PA. The numbers were both unnecessarily high (No. 13990 on page 25, in my case) and, given the sparse crowd and limited program sales, always tantalizingly close to being a winner. I missed by one number, 13889, a free round of golf at the Eagle Creek Country Club.

Attendance for the game, in which free team card sets were given to the first five hundred kids, was announced at 2,703 for the 6,000-capacity stands. But I'd have been surprised if there were one thousand people there. You could clearly hear ball meet leather—not only from a fastball in the catcher's mitt but from a long fly landing in an outfielder's glove.

I hadn't been to a Travelers game since I'd moved to New York twenty years before, but I was in town for my thirtieth high school reunion, and the team was leaving Ray Winder Field after that season for a new stadium being constructed across the river in North Little Rock. The old ballpark, named for an early general manager of the team, was the one constant, since the players were always changing. And for a decade of summers in my early life, the utilitarian concrete and I-beam place served as snack shop, social club, playground, and memory palace.

Not much had changed since then. The ticket booth still dispensed a small two-part orange voucher, which the turnstile attendant separated, returning the half reading RAIN CHECK. The décor of the concession area, just as I remembered it, resembled a 1970s rec room, with its fake wood paneling. The press box, suspended in seeming perilous fashion from the roof, was an open gondola, cooled by ceiling fans. And the men's room, as then, featured one long communal urinal, at which one had to overcome fear of public micturition or else suffer the effects of consuming numerous Sno-Cones and Cokes.

From my seat in the bleachers, I spotted a family friend, Bert, in the box seats, in the same section his family and mine had held season tickets some four decades before. I made my way down (no usher checked my bleacher stub) and sat next to him. He was cooling himself with a miniature fan attached to a water bottle. His son Frank, a high school classmate of mine, shortly joined us.

"Marguerite's over there in the smoking section," said Bert, mentioning a longtime neighboring box-seat holder. "She'll be back shortly." Marguerite was an ardent keeper of her own scorecard, mastering, as I once had, the runic code that documented the game: 6-3 for a ground-out to the shortstop, a shaded-in diamond for a run scored. A month earlier, the last time I'd been in Little Rock, she had come, as had Bert and his family, to the memorial service for my brother, Walt, with whom I'd roamed Ray Winder Field long ago and who had died unexpectedly just after his fiftieth birthday of a severe arterial blockage. Now, some kids about the age we were then sat on the concrete terrace above the dugout, dealing out their free player cards in an invented game.

In those days, I read the box scores in the daily paper and

subscribed to the *Sporting News*, but I had no major-league allegiances. When I was growing up in Little Rock in the nineteen-sixties and seventies, the only professional sports team in town was the Travs, then an affiliate of the St. Louis Cardinals (and now of the even more distant Los Angeles Angels of Anaheim). The Travs had similar uniforms, with the dual redbirds perched on a bat across the chest, the cursive "Travelers" underneath in the style of the parent team's "Cardinals." Some of the better players who came through, like Keith Hernandez, went on to star for the big club, but the association didn't translate for me. I was a Travelers fan; the Cardinals I could take or leave.

A minor-league fan is the most sweetly melancholic of sports fans. We know the players are not really there to win but to perform individually in order to reach the next level. And most of them, at least in Double A, never will move on; their baseball dreams end in places like Little Rock, Altoona, Mobile, and Corpus Christi. Unlike the big-league fans who demand flawlessness from their millionaires, the only froth a bush-league fan gets into is the one on top of his beer. And while Albert Pujols may inspire awe among urbanites with his Olympian skill, the flaws of our struggling prospects and aging has-beens are all too apparent, and we love them more for their faults. The players separated from us by a chicken-wire backstop are just a dropped fly away from jobs like ours, so we can't be too hard on them. In my youth, the worst we might do is call out "Mo-des-to!" naming the franchise in California where an underperforming player would be demoted.

The marginal player who most caught my imagination in my youth was Lenny Boyer, the least talented of the baseball-playing Boyer brothers, three of whom made the majors. A light-hitting, error-prone third baseman, Boyer inspired this bit of doggerel from my eight-year-old poet's pen: Lenny Boyer, Number 11, I sure hope you go to heaven.

This year's Lenny Boyer was a catcher named Brent Del

Chiaro, who was batting .133 and had struck out in more than a third of his eighty-four at-bats. He went down once more on strikes. Bert looked over his shoulder at another fan and said with a good-natured laugh, "But he did it swinging this time."

In that familiar section, I was as soaked in nostalgia as in sweat. From that place in summers past, I'd dash to the dugout fence to plead with the batboy to hand over broken bats. I still have one from a player named Wayne Dees, now apparently a golf-club repairer in Alabama, Google tells me. From those seats, I'd first learned that I would need glasses because I couldn't read the scoreboard, and as I got older, I'd been distracted from the action on the field by the prettiness of the players' wives—and then glad I'd gotten glasses. Out past the left field fence was the Arkansas National Guard's Ricks Armory building, the site of the prom I'd attended as a high school senior with a cheerleader named Susan, who at the reunion later that weekend wouldn't remember me.

As the innings wore on and the humidity soaked the fans and the San Antonio Missions built a 7-2 lead, Bert, Marguerite, and much of the rest of the crowd headed home; most of them had to work the next day, after all. I stuck around, and the Travelers pushed across three runs in the bottom of the eighth to come within two. The management rewarded those who'd remained by announcing that Pabst Blue Ribbon was available at the concession stand for one dollar, and I paid for a beer with the coins in my pocket. In the ninth, the Travs mounted yet another rally, bringing one run home with two on and two out. As the scattered few began to clap in unison—the organist had also gone home—outfielder Matt Pali flied to right to end the game. Del Chiaro, on deck, missed his chance for redemption. The players on base jogged to the dugout and congratulated each other modestly on at least making a game of it. I killed my PBR and stood up to leave.

It was a sweetly melancholic ending. Our team had lost,

yes—by one run, just as my lucky number in the program had missed by one—but it was impossible to feel angry or disappointed. Our flawed players, the eccentric old park, and the intimate, familiar crowd had provided an occasion for empathy, a celebration of the perfectly ordinary even as life cuffs you around: your brother dies too soon, your prom date forgets you, and you strike out more than a third of the time.

And then, on the way out the gate (for the last time), I discovered it was bread night at Ray Winder Field, and everyone who'd stayed got two free loaves to swing in each hand on the way to the parking lot.

Snow Patrol

by Buck Marsh

The temperature was below zero. There was no moon, but we were walking in twenty inches of snow, so you could see fairly well from the snow reflection. After walking two hundred yards or so, I glanced to the rear and here came our engineers, each carrying tank mines—all in dark olive drab overcoats that were visible in the snow for miles, it appeared. It concerned me that we had to come back through the minefield area, but I didn't worry long because I had worse concerns about what lay ahead than what lay behind me. The engineers followed for a little longer, then placed their mines and returned to our lines. Remembering that our briefing Major had said the engineers would advance their minefield to a "safe" distance, I assumed that we were now in an "unsafe" area.

It was 1944, I was twenty years old, and we were stationed in Belgium fighting what would be dubbed the "Battle of the Bulge."

Earlier that evening four of us were summoned to Company Headquarters and introduced to a Major from Battalion Headquarters. He first stated that we were a reconnaissance patrol and not a combat patrol; we were not to engage the enemy. I liked what he said, but he could have saved it: we four GIs had no intention of going out there in the pitch black night to challenge the whole German army in their own backyard. They would probably be upset if they even knew we were there, much less if we started shooting at them.

Our Major proceeded to tell us that we were to go across the five hundred yards of fairly open terrain to our front. This area was covered by our dug-in machine guns as our MLR. After crossing this terrain, we were to intersect a small sunken road, proceed one thousand yards along this road, go through an iron gate, climb a hill, "get comfortable" and look and listen for German movement. This would put us approximately a half mile into enemy territory. The Major also told us that our battalion engineers would be following us at a "safe" distance to extend their tank minefield. He then instructed each of us to remove all personal items from our pockets, keeping our dog tags only. Now this doesn't sound like any big deal—but as you pile up a knife, wallet, ring, and other incidental items, it dawns on you that he is doing this in case you are captured. All of a sudden, these items become very, very personal as you wonder if you will ever see them again.

We were all ready to go, except for one thing. Unlike the Germans, who had been planning this offensive for some time and whose equipment was thoroughly winterized and many of them had snow boots as well as white camouflaged snowsuits, we had no winter gear to speak of.

So, some GIs back in supply took white bed sheets and improvised a "snowsuit." They sewed a hood onto the sheet and sewed strips to tie around both arms, both legs and the waist, covering our entire uniform. I noticed the guy helping me tie my sheet around my arms and legs kept smiling. I asked him what was so damned humorous; it seemed very serious to me. I looked to my rear—there must have been six feet of sheet following after me on the floor. I looked like a five-foot-five bride coming down the church aisle with a ten-foot train! We remedied that by cutting some off. Now we were ready for our "non-combat" patrol.

We were given a ride to our last machine gun outpost and as we walked through this line, were given the sign and countersign for that night. This would be very important on our return to be able to identify ourselves as friendly troops.

Shortly, we came upon the sunken road, just as our Major

had said. It was about six feet wide, but the snow had blown in and was deep. Along each side were earthen banks about head high, covered with thick bushes weighted down with icicles. Our Sgt. Dave Knarr and another GI were in front—one at each side of the sunken road—and myself with the other patrol member to their rear, maybe twenty feet. Walking was terribly slow, with snow up to mid-thigh. I suppose we had gone over halfway toward the iron gate when we heard other people walking toward us. They were not in the sunken road, but at the top, knocking icicles off the bushes as they brushed against them from the outside of the road.

All of us melted into the deep snowdrift down along the sides of our road and waited. Our worst fears were realized as they passed within ten feet of us, mumbling and whispering in German. As I lay in that deep snow, I was most thankful for the GI who had made our funny snowsuits. They were funny no more. It must have taken the German soldiers some five minutes to go by our position—probably there were twenty-five or thirty of them (although one of our patrol later said there were at least a hundred!). We were careful that all had gone by before we crawled up to Dave Knarr's position. We only looked at each other and, finally, someone asked about a drumming noise. It was my heart beating, I told him.

We discussed our situation in very quiet tones and then one guy told Dave Knarr that if Dave wanted to go to that iron gate, as per the Major's instructions, it would be a three-man patrol because he felt that we had accomplished our mission. I pointed out that our Major, during briefing, had designated us a reconnaissance patrol and not a combat patrol. I didn't care about "ambushing" these Germans on their return. We had all been told that the Germans were moving swiftly and not taking any prisoners.

In a short time, all hell broke loose back at our machine gun emplacements. It was obvious that the Germans had made contact with our troops. This firefight with burp guns, machine guns, and hand grenades must have lasted half an hour. While this fight was taking place, we moved one hundred yards or so down the sunken road toward the iron gate, finally finding a place to get out of the sunken road on the side opposite from the Germans' path. We went only forty feet and came upon a rock wall built around a well or spring. This provided us with cover, plus got us out of that road in case the Germans came back down it. We had a clear view of the road and bushes from here.

As we sat behind this stone wall in two feet of snow, no one mentioned being cold; in fact, if the truth were known, all of us were probably sweating. We didn't have to wait too long before we could hear the Germans coming back the same route; only this time, they were not too quiet. The wounded were groaning and talking, while the ones carrying them were grunting and fussing. In their snowsuits, it was hard to see them from our vantage point of sixty or seventy feet. We gave them plenty of time to go by and then Knarr insisted we wait another ten minutes or so.

I was ready to get back to our friendly lines, but I'm sure his decision was the correct one. No other Germans came after this ten-minute wait, so very carefully and quietly we re-entered the sunken road and proceeded toward our lines.

As we came out of the sunken road and started across the open terrain, I completely forgot the minefield. We were all anxious to get into our company area, but concerned about our own GIs shooting us. We came upon a few dead Germans and, at this point, Knarr had us all lie down and he shouted in a very loud voice toward our lines that we were friendly troops. The sign and countersign were exchanged, but still our troops had him give the names of the people in our patrol. Knarr only knew me as "Buck" and when he asked my last name, I told him loud enough to be heard in Liege! Finally, we were told to come forward. In our beautiful "snow-suits" we could not have been mistaken for Germans, with all the flaps, ties, knots, and excess material. I shouldn't laugh about those old bed sheets because they probably saved our lives in that sunken road.

We were hustled off to Company Headquarters to report our recon findings. On the short walk to Headquarters, one of our patrol asked Knarr what he was going to tell the Major we saw. Knarr replied, "Whatever they wanted us to see, we saw!"

As we entered the briefing room, everyone there seemed surprised that we had gotten back with such a fight having taken place. Not many questions were asked. I guess the fight proved that the enemy was close by. And as I walked out of that briefing room and out the door to my foxhole, the most important thing to me was putting that old knife back in my pocket.

The Nesting Loon

by Susan Toone

When we finally met her in the lobby of our hotel, I was crying so hard that I couldn't even focus— our daughter loves to hear how we skipped the part where all the parents hang around to admire their own and others' babies, and instead I grabbed her under my arm like a football and raced back to our room.

I would describe myself as impatient under the best of circumstances, but my two-year wait for Mei Li made impatience one of my core competencies, along with anxiety, despair, agitation, and paranoia. Not only was I a bit long in the tooth, but I convinced myself that even those who had neither the desire nor the paperwork would be blessed with a child—except me. I would be denied my heart because it had to be obvious to everyone that I wasn't mother material. I wasn't the kind of woman who stopped to coo at every baby, who loved all children and felt a rush of maternal tenderness at their appearance. I thought far too many of them were no-neck monsters who sucked up their parents' time, energy, and disposable income. In fact, I had never had any desire for children until I met John, who once told my mother that after our initial introduction, I basically said, "I'm Susan, and I want to have your children."

Although we decided on her name four months into the wait, I did not buy anything for her: no clothes, no toys, no crib, no music, no books (although I did break down and buy *The Owl and the Pussycat* a few months before bringing her home). Why bother? She would never come home to me. She would go to one of those mothers you read about who is not only musical and artistic and able to host perfect tea parties, but is also the earth mother, who makes you feel as if you've known her all your life upon first meeting her in her cozy kitchen where all the neighborhood mothers and children gather to bask in her glow and eat her homemade cookies. That mother would be waiting calmly, humming while she embroidered sheets, curtains, and mother-daughter outfits. She would perfect her Mandarin during the wait. She would be recording lullabies she wrote to soothe her little one to sleep. She would be worried only that she wouldn't be able to finish hand-carving the rocking chair and cradle, blocks, and matching chess and checkerboard set. She made me look like Medea, except I didn't dress as well.

Among my worries in case a miracle happened and we did bring her home, were, in no special order: she won't like us, we won't like her, she'll be ugly, I won't be able to really love her and vice versa, she'll cry all the time and I'll discover that I don't want to be a mother and then it's too late and I'm stuck with her, I'm WAY too old, we don't have enough money and she'll end up working at King McTaco the rest of her life because we can't afford college for her, I was going to have to return to work and what's the point of flying across the Big Pond to bring home a baby and then abandon her to strangers at day care, we'll both lose our jobs and be homeless. And these don't include the really crazy ones.

I joined an online group for waiting parents, and although it gave me great comfort, it also fueled my madness in many respects. I took every rumor to heart and would call our agency and demand to know to know why they hadn't told me that China had stopped all adoptions for women in Arkansas or that the wait had changed from an average of one year to twelve. I think now how they must have snorted and rolled their eyes at others in the office, mouthing "It's HER" as they patiently (but with no success) tried to soothe my last raw nerve. I wanted to scream and run headfirst into a brick wall when they told me that when the time was right, I would become the mother of the baby who was meant to be mine—it was all part of God's divine plan. Yeah, right.

And then, the strangest thing happened. As I chatted up our six-month-old daughter Mei Li in the hotel room that first day, I realized that this baby, all 11 ¾ pounds of her, had banished my malevolent emotional companions of the past year. The truth of this being part of God's divine plan immediately washed over me, although I didn't think in those terms until much later. At last, there were only three of us in the room (four if you count bliss).

By the next day, John said that she didn't yet know we were her parents, but she had no doubt we were the best nannies she'd ever had.

Now I'm the one who says essentially the same thing about God's divine plan to waiting parents, but I preface my remarks with "I know you will want to smack me for saying this and will probably find no comfort in it now, but you must believe me."

My friend Kristy, extraordinary friend, sage, counselor and godmother to my children, copied me on this email she sent to our mutual friends, Nancy and Mark, in response to their dazed announcement that their heart and soul—a seven-month old baby girl—was waiting for them in China.

> *Shopping, packing, fretting, shopping more, changing what you plan to pack—I still remember this from Mei Li's arrival. The funniest part is at absolute zero hour when it is time to complete the packing and head to the airport, Susan decides she has to shave and tan her legs. I finished her packing—she made herself beautiful for her new daughter. I guess that was her way of "nesting."*

Neither John nor I remember the incident: it has been

almost twelve years since that crucial leg-shaving. My overall memory is of a frenzied madness. I was consumed with thoughts—many of them deranged—of bringing home my baby.

Among all the great pictures taken at the airport on our arrival home, one reflects perfectly my contentment: I am just coming off the plane, radiating happiness and preparing to hoist her up to our adoring crowd of relatives and friends.

I am still buzzing with excitement for Nancy and Mark, although something shocking has hit me: when the love of their life turns nine, mine will be eighteen—a startling and unwelcome reminder of how close she is to leaving the nest I waited so long to create for her.

Fishing with Vitale

by Nathan McKinney

On a cool December morning my little brother Mark and I threw our stuff in the back of my truck and drove from Sherwood, Arkansas to Baton Rouge, Lousiana. We were looking forward to fishing with my friend Eddie, who is quite possibly the best fisherman on the planet. I'd been fishing with Eddie a bunch, but this was the first time for my little brother.

As we drove, I told Mark just how good it was fixing to be. "We'll catch fish!" I said. "We'll bring the ice chest back full of fillets, and I mean full."

Mark's eyes got big.

"We fish three days. We catch our limit three days."

"Do you think?" he asked.

"Oh, yeah. We'll slay 'em."

Mark smiled. "Speckled trout?"

I nodded.

"Do they fight?" he asked.

"They'll pull your arms off."

I glanced at him; Mark was about to cry.

I call Mark my "little" brother, but we were exactly the same size and I was only two years older. Mark and I had fought bitterly growing up. At times we hated one another. We shouted, cussed, hit, kicked. It was—ugly. But I left home for college and things changed. We became civil. We started hanging out together; and occasionally enjoying it. By the time I graduated from college, we were friends. We both got married and our wives became friends. One day I realized that, at age thirty-two, my little brother had become my best friend.

We spent the night with Eddie, got up and drove south to the marsh. We stopped at Thibodeaux's Store to buy some food for the day. The proprietor of the place was an old, wrinkled Cajun who, at 5:30 in the morning, smelled a little like shrimp and a lot like whiskey. He greeted us with a grin revealing a solitary gold tooth. We got enough to keep us fed and watered; it was at least eight dollars of food.

Tooth, he stared at our food and his lips moved like he was adding up the total in his head. "T'ree dolla."

"He's lit," Eddie whispered.

Mark said, "That can't be right."

"Two dolla."

We were in a hurry, so I threw a ten on the counter.

We got out the door and Tooth called out to us, "De ga' war' he be bah in de bayou. He han' fa' hund dolla foin. You don bot yo'loisan, eh?"

We looked at Eddie. Since he was from Baton Rouge, maybe he could interpret. Eddie said, "He's lit."

We put the boat in the water and motored down Bayou Barre. The marsh of Terrebonne Parish is a labyrinth of bayous, canals and shallow lakes surrounded by stiff, golden, marsh grass, interrupted only by an occasional chicken tree or oil rig. The water is brackish and the air is thick and pungent. Brown pelicans, blue herons, and various species of gulls are everywhere. Shrimp dance on the surface of the water. I got excited; Mark was about to pee in his britches.

We started fishing, throwing plastic cockaho jigs. We fished cuts and dead end canals for three hours. We caught— nothing.

Eddie said, "The wind is keeping the tide up. The fish won't turn on until the tide turns."

We fished hard for three more hours. We caught—nothing.

Eddie said, "If the wind lets up, we'll catch some specs."

Mark looked at me. I detected some doubt in his eyes.

We fished hard for three more hours. We caught—nothing.

The sun set, we loaded the boat and checked into the Sugar Bowl Motel. The Sugar Bowl catered to fishermen. We figured that out by the hand-written sign on the door, "No clean fish on floor. No fry fish in room. No smoke in bed." We had no fish to clean, no fish to fry and we didn't smoke; we went to bed.

The next morning we stopped at Thibodeaux's. Tooth smelled like shrimp and whiskey. We got eight dollars worth of food. Tooth said, "T'ree dolla."

Mark protested.

"Two dolla."

I left him a ten.

Tooth hollered at us, "De ga war he be bah in de bayou. He han' fa' hund dolla foin. You don bot yo' loisan, eh?"

We fished Bayou Barre for three hours. We fished Wonder Lake for three hours. We fished the weir for three hours. The wind kept the tide up. We actually caught some Sheepshead, but Eddie considered them trash fish and he made us throw them back. We didn't catch any specs. None.

My ice chest was empty and Mark looked discouraged. Maybe he didn't believe my stories of catching boatloads of fish. Maybe my little brother was losing faith in me.

The Sugar Bowl Motel had ESPN on TV! At the time, ESPN was still a novelty and Dick Vitale was their voice of college basketball. For the uninitiated, Dick Vitale is a New Jersey Yankee that talks with a distinct nasal quality. He gets excited and he's subject to wild hyperbole which can range from funny to obnoxious. That night he was funny, or at least we thought so. Oh, man did we laugh. We went to sleep laughing.

The next morning we stopped at Thibodeaux's. Tooth smelled like shrimp and whiskey. We did the, "T'ree dolla'/Two dolla'" routine. Tooth delivered his Cajun soliloquy. Then Eddie, with great ceremony, opens his wallet and shows his fishing license to Tooth. He told me and Mark to do likewise. Tooth studied all three of our licenses. Then he grinned real wide, revealing a second gold tooth. Oh, my goodness! I had given Tooth a false nickname!

In the boat, Eddie explained that he finally understood what Tooth was saying: "The game warden, he be bad in de bayou. He hand five hundred dollar fine. You done bought your license, eh?" Why, Tooth was just trying to help us avoid trouble! Bless his heart.

We fished till noon and caught a few throw-away Sheepshead. No speckled trout. We were so tired, so discouraged. We stopped fishing and just looked around for a moment. The marsh can be one of the most serene and beautiful places on earth. The sunrises are warm; the sunsets are brilliant, rich and so colorful. Both sunrise and sunset can last for hours. And we had been here, surrounded by this beauty for two and a half days and we hadn't caught the first speckled trout! Forget the beauty, where were the fish?!!

Eddie sadly announced "Fellows, let's call it a trip."

I looked at Mark. His head was hung low.

We started putting our gear away when, I swear, the wind just died and I noticed the slightest little movement in the tide. I threw my cockaho jig toward the back of the canal. I felt a sudden THUMP! Then a hard jerk and pull. A 21-inch trout leaped in the air. Without thinking, I did my best imitation of Dick Vitale, "It's unbelievable, Baby!"

Eddie threw out and instantly his rod tip bounced. He yelled, "It's dunkaroo time!"

Mark threw out and three seconds later he yelled out, "He's a prime-time-player!"

We had three big specs on the line at the same time! We got them in the boat and did it again, each time mocking Vitale when the fish hit the jig. We caught trout on nearly every cast, with the strictly observed rule that you had to announce your catch with a Dick Vitale phrase.

If the law had been in the marsh that day, they would've locked us up. We didn't care. We were catching fish! Folks, it was pure joy for two hours.

And then they just turned off. Over. So we cleaned the fish and headed back.

We celebrated that night by eating at Ralph and Cackoo's in Baton Rouge. We had crawfish ettouffée; it was good. Mark was so tired that he actually nodded off asleep between bites a few times.

On the trip back home, I asked him, "You want to do this again?"

He looked at me funny and said, "Are you kidding me?!"

We talked about the next fishing trip for months. We circled some dates on the calendar and we let Eddie know we were coming in a few weeks.

The phone call came early on a Saturday morning. "Mark took sick last night. We called an ambulance. We don't know what's wrong, but it's bad. Real bad."

I jumped in my truck and drove fast, but spinal meningitis took him before I arrived.

I've been fishing in the marsh with Eddie at least twenty times since, bringing home an ice chest full of filets nearly every time. The fishing trip to Terrebonne Parish has become an annual event that I look forward to all year.

My little brother never went fishing again.

Funerals, Shopping Trips: What's the Difference?

by Joy Rockenbach

My friends Suzanne and Elaine quickly jumped in the back seat of the Nissan Maxima, which left me up front with Mr. Charles. Not one who abides silence well, I started in on Mr. Charles to tell us his favorite funeral food. I quickly glanced in the back seat just in time to see eyes rolling. This coming from at least one woman who had said her favorite funeral food was paté. Please.

This adventure, er, trip to a funeral began when my friend and fellow Mississippi Deltan, Debbie's father, died. Just because I was now a sophisticated citizen of Little Rock in no way meant that I was so beyond my raising as not to show up for the funeral in Greenville, Mississippi. Besides, one got to Greenville via Lake Village and Lake Village means a trip to Paul Michael's, one of the most famous home décor stores in the country, no matter who has died! Two other friends deemed it important to support our friend via Paul Michael's as well—bless their hearts.

We set out early the morning of said adventure, er, funeral. I kissed my husband good-bye and popped into the back seat of Suzanne's trusty old Taurus station wagon. Suzanne, who was reared in New York, is the mother of seven incredibly accomplished young men and women—the kind that just make you want to slap your own no-good offspring for not being fighter pilots and surgeons too. Suzanne is also the kindest, most nurturing friend anyone could ever have. Elaine, on the other hand, is truly a lady of refined Southern culture.

Although not born of it I suspect, Elaine had acquired the essence of charming Southern femininity. She was always immaculately turned out for any occasion with the appropriate pumps, polish, and pearls. I looked forward to spending the day with these two women.

Besides a funeral meant funeral food and I do enjoy a good funeral buffet. A respectable Delta funeral would have fried chicken—not the kind you "pick up" but the kind the church ladies stay behind and fix so as to be ready after the service. And possibly there would be banana pudding—not your lazy Jell-o variety but the kind with the custard boiled on the stove until it was yellow and thick with eggs and vanilla. Yessir, it was going to be a good day!

Somewhere in all the chatting and musing about the food buffet, I occasionally thought I smelled oil burning. But I also drove an old model Taurus myself, whose odometer had flipped at least three times and whose "check engine" light stayed on all the time. It would also just stop, I am convinced, when it got too hot and tired. We, me and it, would rest a while and it would start and go on until it got tired again. So, needless to say, I did not pay much attention to a little ole burning oil smell until . . . somewhere between Pine Bluff and McGeehee, I was fidgeting in the back seat and drinking too much water when I noticed the oil light was on. Now, I might currently be a highly-cultured and educated Southern woman, but my Daddy drummed into me that when that light came on you stop. They don't call it the idiot light for nothing.

So, I brought up to Suzanne that I think the oil light might have just come on and she said, "Yeah, it's been doing that ever since I had the oil changed the other day."

"Maybe we should stop and have it looked at," I said.

Fortunately we were right close to a little service station a few miles the other side of McGeehee. Suzanne ran in and ran right back out to say they don't seem to offer any services other than cigarettes and beer and we would need to go back to McGeehee for any oil.

Then Elaine said, "Well, I vote for pointing it in the direction we are heading and going as fast as we can."

And I said . . . well, I can't tell you what I said because I had my funeral suit on and it wasn't nice.

About twenty-five feet pointed in the direction we were heading, the engine locked up and the car came to a complete stop. I capped my water bottle. Suzanne whipped out her phone with AAA on speed dial and commenced to telling some twelve-year-old little girl sitting in Wisconsin whereabouts we were on Highway 65 South so they could send a tow truck. Elaine, ever more practical, whipped out her phone with Paul Michael's on speed dial and said, "Hi, we are three ladies from Little Rock, Arkansas coming shopping today at Paul Michael's and our car just quit on the side of the road. Is there anybody who can come get us?"

In less than fifteen minutes a nice new Nissan Maxima pulled up with a tow truck close behind. A man with "James" stitched on a blue work shirt got out of the tow truck, shaking his head and clucking his tongue as he looked under the hood. His daddy, Mr. Charles, got out of the Maxima and said he would be proud to take us on into Lake Village in his car since you could not expect three nice white ladies to ride in a tow truck.

And that's how I ended up in the front seat with Mr. Charles while the other two sniggered in the backseat.

While we had been waiting for Paul Michael's to "send someone" we had called our friend Debbie whose father was lying in a coffin to tell her our dilemma—like she didn't already have enough trouble. She in turn hollered to someone that her friends from Little Rock had a car broken down and they needed a ride from Lake Village to the church in Greenville. She came back on the line and said the funeral home would be sending a car. Great. First a tow truck, and now the possibility of a hearse. Could it get any better?

We were assured that someone from the funeral home would meet us in Lake Village or be there just shortly. When we got to the home of the tow truck and new Nissan Maxima in Lake Village, Elaine, while gently fondling her pearls, asked Mr. Charles if she might avail herself of his facilities. I could have just died! We are talking *Sanford and Son*! We are talking junk yard of junk yards! I am sure I saw the bodies of old Chevy trucks and at least one gremlin out there! But no, Elaine has to go to the "facilities" and since we are now very close to my home turf, I figure I better go with her.

Well, shut my mouth! We entered one of the nicest bathrooms I have nearly ever seen. I wish I'd had time to take a bath. It was huge—bigger than my kitchen even. It had plants and a skylight and tub big enough for four friends, easy. The only thing a little disconcerting was the fur-lined commode seat.

By the time Elaine and I came back out, Bubba Earl from the funeral home rolled up in a Jeep Cherokee with a case of Corona in the back.

Well, we made it to the funeral and there was fried chicken AND banana pudding at the funeral buffet. In case you are thinking, "Wait, what about the car and how did you get back to Little Rock?"

Honey, we were in the Delta. We sold the car to Debbie's brother's new wife who owned a salvage yard just below Greenville (she wasn't really new, they had been married for years but she just wasn't the old wife) and then Debbie sent us all back home in her car with her oldest boy and his wife with strict orders to stop at Paul Michael's in Lake Village, which he did. When I got home late that evening, my husband was on the roof (he had said he was going to stay up there until the last administration was out of office, but that is another whole story all by itself). He hollered down, "Did you all have a good time?" I just rolled my eyes and said, "Honey, get down here, you are NOT going to believe what happened!"

Stop that Paperman!

by Tim Bennett

Cahpoht! Put it on the cahpoht! Stop that paperman!" the woman screamed hysterically, arms waving like a windmill. She stood at the end of the deeply rutted dirt driveway filled with chuckholes that a family of four could live in comfortably. Acting like I couldn't hear her, I poked the newspaper through the half-open car window; it limply plopped down on the ground as I sped away to the next delivery.

It had come to this. A few months out of college and there I was, the "Assistant Circulation Manager" of the *Ruston Daily Leader* newspaper in Ruston, Louisiana (where it is pronounced loozie-ana). By taking a job in circulation, I had hoped to eventually work my way over to the newsroom.

My whole life I had loved newspapers since I started reading them at eight years old. I read not only the comics but also Ann Landers, Heloise, and all of the features I could find. Besides news stories like the grisly Tate-LaBianca murders committed by the Manson family, the papers also offered AP and UPI wire service stories with reports from all over the country and the world. My family had daily subscriptions to the *Los Angeles Times* as well as the local *Southeast Daily News* along with the Sunday edition of the *Herald-Examiner*.

The *Arkansas Gazette,* the oldest newspaper west of the Mississippi, was waiting for me when my family and I moved to Arkansas while I was in high school. In college I worked for *The Bray*, the student voice of the Southern Arkansas University Mule Riders, where I wrote a weekly column, features, news, and even helped to "put the paper to bed" before it was sent off to be printed. I loved everything about a newspaper.

Except circulation. Now I was delivering newspapers of currently unmanned motor routes in Northeast Louisiana, counting out stacks of newspapers for each delivery person, preparing newspapers for mail subscriptions, trying to motivate carriers not to quit, and handling complaints from aggravated subscribers.

The first few phone calls were not a gentle introduction into the world of customer service.

"I haven't gotten my paper today and I want to know hwah!" the elderly woman declared. Her accent intrigued me, especially how she switched the h and the w when she said "why." It sounded like a baby with asthma crying, "Hwah!"

"Yes Ma'am," I responded. "We'll get one right out to you. Can I have your name and address?"

Sometimes a customer's call turned darkly sarcastic. "Are y'all puttin' out a paper today?" asked one grumpy, deep-voiced man. "Uh, yes Sir, the paper is out today." "Well, I hadn't gotten it," he shot back disgustedly. Once a man bitterly announced, "I haven't gotten my G-D paper." "Uh, can you tell me who your carrier is? "Ah don't know, some (racial epithet) wench throws it," he responded venomously. He was referring to Route 8, a sweet, soft-spoken lady trying to make a living. I slammed the phone receiver down like it would burn me if I held it any longer.

When customers had complaints, the person handling the call would write down the complaint and accompanying information on a little pink slip and place it with the newspapers for the carrier to pick up when he or she arrived in the early afternoon. Occasionally, there were gaps between the intended delivery and receipt of the newspaper. The carrier might throw the newspaper a little too high and it might end up on the roof, a dog might run off with it, someone might steal the newspaper, or it might remain in the tall grass, hidden in the yard like some Easter egg.

Apparently, the *Ruston Daily Leader* had one carrier with a lot of personality. A short blond guy with a fast sports car, Ray kept getting complaints from Mrs. Opal Jones at 423 Pine St., who daily called to report that she was not getting her paper. Ray knew he was throwing it each day. One, two, three, four, the little pink slips kept coming back around like a bad T.V. commercial.

Finally one Wednesday, Ray had had enough. On "extra paper day," the newspaper gave the carriers fifty, seventy-five, one hundred extra papers to throw on their routes to lure customers into signing up for a subscription. Although they inserted ads, rolled, rubber-banded, and finally threw the extra merchandise, the carriers didn't get any extra money, so everyone was already in a bad mood.

Ray came to retrieve his newspapers from the long wooden counter, looked at the nagging, inaccurate pink slip, gathered up the papers, and promptly dumped all of the extra ones at 423 Pine St. Mrs. Opal Jones definitely got her paper that day. Ray lost his job, but he was ready to go anyway. The story was told and retold in circulation from time to time and savored like a guilty snack.

Now my own collection of pink slips began to pile up from a Mrs. Ronnie Lee Hendrix, who wanted her paper on the carport. It said so right on the slip under her name and address, "put the paper on the carport."

That request got all over me: I was having to fill in on this particular route because the carrier had unexpectedly quit, so my job had been reduced to glorified paperboy. At least the main boss lent me his car to drive, though unlike Ray's, it was a compact, pale yellow Ford, definitely a family vehicle.

On this particular dirt road, which looped around the neighborhood, I had to be extra careful: you could knock the car out of alignment by just looking at the deeply pitted road. I got aggravated when I realized that the long driveway that led to Mrs. Hendrix's house atop a little hill was in even worse shape than the road. The pink slip might as well have said, "put paper on a silver platter," or "put paper on carport after creating origami animal figures out of it." It just wasn't going to happen.

After the first few calls brought no response, she was ready. "Cahpoht, put the paper on the cahpoht!" Mrs. Hendrix screamed. I acted like her arm waving was like a friendly greeting and I responded with a quick wave while tossing the paper one millimeter over the property line. Then I hit the gas and got out of there.

This scene was repeated two more times. Finally, Mrs. Hendrix came running out and as I took off after throwing the little cylinder of newsprint, she lost it. She reared back and balled up her fists and let loose a deep, guttural scream like a wild animal, a cougar or a panther. Her knees actually briefly met as she released her cry of tortured, anguished frustration. The hairs stood up on the back of my neck.

By then I was wondering if I might be pursued by a pickup truck full of neighborhood toughs demanding to know what I had done to the tormented soul. I actually did feel a little guilty. Mrs. Hendrix's overreaction was a little crazy; it's not like I came from social services to seize her baby or from some company to unjustly shut off a utility without warning. Still, to know I had caused another human being discomfort or pain was not a good feeling.

I hope that now a nice asphalt-covered, paved road leads up to a smooth concrete driveway, where a newspaper is being retrieved daily from that carport at the Hendrix home, maybe by Mrs. Hendrix herself, who obviously loved to read a newspaper like I did.

The Lake

by Hope Coulter

On the way to the lake, there's one place where the road goes through an orchard and the trees arch over in a high, green, lacy vault, and it's like you're in a chariot, rolling under. Me and Phoebe and Mimi call it the Gates of Fairyland. Their father says, "Almost there, girls!" Then we smell it—part fish, part wet, caked leaves. It's Lake St. John, an oxbow lake, left behind when the Mississippi River changed direction. But we just call it the lake.

The station wagon turns into the drive, nosing between banana trees, and there's the house, same as ever—with its siding the dull green of hospital scrubs, and its flat, pebbled-asphalt roof, and its back yard of sticker patches sloping down to the lake.

Which, after the car is unloaded, we run to. Drape ourselves over the pier rail. "It's like melted glass," says Phoebe. "Pink and gold." A wide, polished table, reflecting the sky. When a skier goes by, far away, the waves start up and relax like our heartbeats.

Inside there's a TV with bunny-ears antenna that only gets Monroe. The yellow-pine paneling swims with brown ovals like ghosts' mouths. Framed on the wall is a child's painting of a sailboat, with the words "Slaying, slaying, over the bounding main." I am eleven myself and have known how to spell sailing as long as I can remember.

Next morning after pancakes we go to the pier and wait for a grownup to come, so we can swim.

Here, at last, comes Uncle Harry. I call him that even

though he's not my uncle. He has on a terrycloth bathrobe, a plaid bathing suit, socks, and canvas slip-ons. His legs look thinner than you would think. I'm used to seeing him either in his surgery scrubs, or in a jacket and tie, like at Phoebe and Mimi's dance recitals, or in these Mexican wedding shirts he wears to parties, that don't have to be tucked in.

He and Aunt Peggy are my parents' oldest friends. They go back to college and, in the men's case, med school—some kind of rushed-up program because it was wartime. They tell stories about wild parties at Tulane. Once, not our fathers but some other boys, they pushed a piano out the window. The new doctors graduated one Friday and took their boards on Saturday. My parents were getting married on the Monday. But my father was in such a daze he couldn't pack for his honeymoon. Harry said, "Having trouble, Tom?"—nicely—and emptied Daddy's dresser drawers one by one into a pillowcase and handed it to him and said, "Here. You're packed."

So Mimi and Phoebe are like my sisters. And with great affection I watch Uncle Harry at the helm of their speedboat, putt-putting out of the boathouse and around the pier. He'll pull us behind that boat all day if we ask him. His face is pink and he fans with his navy captain's cap, then smiles as he taps a cigarette into his palm. "Who's first?" he says. "Hopie, you gonna try to get up?"

Once Aunt Peggy gets in, to tread water near me, boosting and coaching, I do. After five or six wipeouts, on one try I tighten my legs and rise through the roaring spray and find myself standing. I'm doing it. Skiing. Skidding a thousand miles an hour over a bumpy floor of water. Mimi and Phoebe wave and whoop. People are on their docks and piers, watching me pass, thinking, There goes a skier.

That night company comes: friends and relatives who live nearby, some uncles and a blond aunt, and cousins, sunburned and joking, filling the doorframes. It's all golden-brown, the paneled room, fried catfish, hush puppies, and amber drinks. Uncle Harry reigns at the table, his arms folded over his belly. Sometimes his face breaks into a v-shaped smile and he tucks his chin, laughing, reaching for his Benson & Hedges. Sometimes he's serious, arching his eyebrows over grave blue eyes. To the men he says, "How in the world are you?" The women lean over to kiss him and say "Mwwah!" with their lips pursed out. He says, "Love you, baby!" Phoebe and Mimi and I fall asleep on our cots on the porch, but the grown-up noise lasts way into the night.

Next day, though, Uncle Harry pads to the bathroom with squinched eyes, and only croaks when we say good morning. Behind the bathroom door we hear the long stream of him peeing. We eye each other, not quite daring to laugh.

He goes back to bed and reappears hours later with a book under his arm, saying he's headed to the pier house to read. When we beg, he changes his mind and agrees to drive the boat. First, he says, he needs his hat and dark glasses; a beer; a towel for his neck; and some aspirin, which turn out to be in Aunt Peggy's purse.

It's hot and dazzling bright. Mimi jumps into the boat, which is tied to the pier, and starts unclipping ropes. As her dad steps in, a wave moves the boat—only slightly, but enough to throw him off. He sways like a tree. For a second he regains his balance. Another wave swells, widening the space between the pier and the side of the boat like a wedge of pie someone is deciding to cut bigger and bigger, and he topples into the water.

He comes up sputtering dammits. Still, we're relieved. It has been a while since he did much swimming, and as he says, "My favorite activities, unfortunately for my physique, are sedentary."

Mimi hooks a ladder over the gunwale. Uncle Harry scrabbles one foot onto the bottom rung, but then can't launch his stomach any higher. A mew of a snicker escapes from Phoebe.

He cusses again. "Mimi, help me out here, baby." "Daddy! Who do you think put this ladder out?" Every time he makes some headway, squeezing his knee into his tummy, his weight twists the ladder and raises one side. Once he rises as far as the second rung. Water streams from his inside-out pocket. Mimi, crouched in the tipping boat, catches my eye and Phoebe's. We fight the laughs, but they keep on trying to bubble up.

Uncle Harry plops backward like a turtle and paddles around to the pier ladder, which is slimy with algae but at least is sturdy and stays put. There he ascends deliberately, gazing across the lake with a stern expression like an explorer taking in new vistas.

"D'you lose your sunglasses?" says Mimi. He gives her a look, then squelches onto the bench. "Yes." "Thank goodness the boat key floats." Phoebe smiles and holds it up. "But your cigarettes and lighter? And your beer?" He's panting too hard to talk.

Mimi spots the hat near the reeds, so we three jump in and race to it and hold it up together like a trophy. Only the braid is slightly bedraggled.

Late that night I wake up in the chilly, lake-smelling air. Mimi and Phoebe are humped in their beds beside me. Now and then a lapping sound comes from the mist over the water. And there's the moon, like a white doubloon. That makes a poem. Our parents went to Mardi Gras last year and brought back a bunch of doubloons and beads. Me and Mimi and Phoebe used my old wagon to play parade. We'd heard about women flashing their breasts, so we lifted our shirts to show our pale chests, strutting and hollering, "Hey Mister, throw me something!" and jumping for the sailing coins and beads— cracking up the whole time.

Inside, now, the grownups are quiet. I'm sorry I have to be one someday. I wish it could stay like this. I don't know what's going to happen, but I have foreboding. I can't see Uncle Harry lie down one summer's day, on his own operating table, with nurses and doctors frantic over him, some of them the very boys who pushed a piano out the window so long ago, crying and trying and failing to keep him alive—can't see their golden friends lapsing one by one—can't see the babies, and the men, and the far far miles. But I sense it out there. Somehow I know. I'll be struggling one day in some dark lake, the likes of which I can barely imagine. Behind me I'll feel the prop of Aunt Peggy's legs, and as the water plows back against me I'll look up to see my friends, their hair whipping in the daylight, their thin arms raised above their heads. "You can do it!" they'll cheer, and that's what will pull me up—the sight of them hauling me forward, out of the rolling wake, to something like standing. Like flight.

A First Time for Everything

by John Wells

I'll always remember the first time I was arrested. The year was 1963 and the place was 12th and University in Little Rock, Arkansas. It was then and there that a very large policeman took me and my best friend into custody. He put us in the back of his patrol car and took us downtown. I was in the third grade. My co-defendant Rick was in the first.

This all happened in our cozy little neighborhood appropriately called Oak Forest, which was carved out of the dense Arkansas fauna, and where all of the houses had at least one huge oak tree in the yard. There wasn't much need for swing sets. They were no competition for hanging a rope off an oak limb with a tire or a stuffed bag on the end. At the time I lived with my mother's nervous sister, Aunt Sammie, and her husband Uncle Bill. Note that when it came to discipline around our house, Aunt Sammie was the decider and Uncle Bill was the hit man. Many a day I dreaded five o'clock. Her judgment rendered, my sentence would be carried out upon his arrival.

Oak Forest grew from its origins on Fair Park almost all the way to the southeast corner of 12th and Hayes. The last little corner of forest survived into the seventies. Rick and I knew every square inch of that patch of woods. We were full of adventure as we trekked the pathways of this half-acre jungle. On more than one occasion our adventures resulted in a broken bone or a cut requiring stitches. Not a single time did it ever happen to me, mind you. When it came to calamity, it was always Rick that required medical attention. One time his parents actually curtailed our friendship for his own safety. Yet, like most kids, we eventually became bored with our conquest of Oak Forest, and that led to mischief. In the old days there was a small gas station at the intersection. In its heyday in the fifties, there were uniformed attendants that filled your tank and checked your tires. If you needed your brakes done or your oil changed, there were two bays to choose from. They even had one of those rubber hoses that rang a bell when you drove over it.

But now modern times had set in. It was the sixties. Hayes Street was now University Avenue, and by 1963 the gas station had long since been idle. There was a sign out front that said: "Closed for rebuilding." To the concrete thinking of third grader, "rebuilding" meant it would be torn down, and then rebuilt. I pictured cranes with wrecking balls pulverizing this poor little structure. I thought, shoot, if they were going to tear it down anyway, we might as well have some fun busting it up a bit in the meantime, right?

At first Rick and I were very cautious. We hurled rocks at the high mounted windows from behind a small chain-link fence that separated the service station from the woods. The range from fence to windows proved to be problematic. Our rocks just weren't producing the desired effect and there were only so many of them. Across the fence there were plenty of rocks, and the range was much more conducive to our pre-adolescent arms. Slowly but surely we became emboldened enough to stand out in the open and fire away. On those rare occasions when we actually broke a pane of glass, we celebrated. That sound was SO COOL.

Then one Sunday afternoon, in the middle of our fun, someone called in the heat. And when I say "in the middle of our fun," I mean that I was in full wind-up when the officer rounded the corner. I cleverly dropped the rock while my hand was still behind my neck. You know the technique, the one that just says, "I was just taking a moment to freshen up my hair."

The officer took control of the crime scene and began to interview his two "persons of interest." His investigation produced the question: what should one do with these two little vandals? At first he threatened to call our parents and tell them how bad we'd been. "OH NO, PLEASE, NOT THAT!!!" He then got on the radio, and the voice on the other end said, "Bring 'em in."

"NO, NO, NO—TELL OUR PARENTS, TELL OUR PARENTS!"

To no avail, we were soon in custody, headed downtown to the place where they take villains like us. "Will we have to go to juvenile detention?" I asked.

"Probably" he replied.

I had no idea what or where juvenile detention was, but I'd heard about it and I did not want to go there.

At the police station we were placed in a room and left by ourselves. We began to discuss the depth of the excrement we were now standing in. It turned out that this free flow of conversation between suspects was not the proper protocol for prisoners in custody, which became evident when the policeman returned and angrily separated us to the far corners of the room.

I recall at that moment remembering about how much I hated *Lassie*, not the dog so much as the television show. The reason I hated *Lassie* was that Rick was mesmerized by it. Once it came on, we could not talk, we could not go outside, we could not play at all. He was frozen in time until the last credit rolled. There at the police station I remember noticing that it was six o'clock, and thinking that I'd much rather be at Rick's house watching *Lassie* than to be sitting there in the pokey.

I also recall the officer calling our homes. Aunt Sammie was a bit on the nervous side by nature, and unfortunately for her, she was the one that answered the phone. She did not have what it took to handle a phone call that started out, "This is the Little Rock Police. We are calling in regards to John . . . ”

That is the last thing she heard. She shed that phone like it was on fire. Uncle Bill took over at that point. He would have to be the one to sort out my complex legal issues.

Without question, I knew that, decider or no decider, this escapade would lead to the thrashing of all thrashings.

After we got sprung, Uncle Bill and I headed to the car. Once there, he and I sat for a bit and discussed the events of the day.

“I bet that was pretty scary,” he said.

I nodded to confirm his hypothesis.

“You know, I don’t think I can top that. I think what you've been through is enough. If you haven’t learned your lesson, nothing I do will change that. We’re going to let this one go.”

Really? That’s it? No thrashing? No time out? I’m not even GROUNDED?

In that moment, a man that was not even a blood relative performed the most amazing feat of parenting I would ever experience. He stood aside as life, along with the LRPD, taught me a very valuable lesson. And you know what? It worked. I have not been arrested since.

It turned out that on this particular Sunday night, Uncle Bill was the best father an eight-year-old ex-con could ever have hoped for.

Broken

by Laura Rakes

Maybe it was the way his words spilled out of his mouth like gravel stuck in molasses; maybe it was the cast on his leg; maybe it was his mouth that hung open, slightly ajar; maybe it was the large, Frankenstein's-monster-like scar that ran the entire length of the right hemisphere of his head; maybe it was the gaping tracheotomy hole; maybe it was the fact that he was sitting in his wheelchair in a surgical oncology waiting room. Whatever it was, it made me feel deep sorrow for this man and his wife, who stood relaxed and committed by his side.

I tried not to stare, but it was really hard not to. He just had so many bad things going for him, and I needed to soak his state into my consciousness so I could understand and properly react with humble graciousness. After all, I was just here for a follow up with the surgeon who removed my gallbladder. Four one-inch-long scars on my abdomen were the only evidence. But this man, this man and his wife—It was almost too much to bear when the wife pushed his wheelchair to the end of the row of seats in which I was sitting.

As the two settled into my comfort zone, I busied myself with Facebook on my phone. "So grateful for me and my family's health, and praying for those who sit in the surgical oncology waiting room." My status updated to reflect my current mood and to allow me to vent about the poor man at the end of the row. Of course, what I really wanted to do was stand up in my chair and announce to the entire clinic that here sits a man who deserves sorrow! The rest of us have nothing to complain about! Oh, but I didn't. My post on

Facebook would have to suffice as a more technically advanced, less assertive equivalent of what I actually wanted to say.

Despite the discomfort his presence caused me, the Broken Man and his wife sat beside me, she slowly grazing through a six-month-old fashion magazine and he staring blankly through the plate-glass windows on the opposite end of the waiting area.

I pretended to check Facebook again. I pretended to check my email for the third time. I pretended to be typing something of some importance into my phone. I slowly came to the realization that I couldn't ignore him. I was the only patient close in proximity to them, and judging by the other patients' waits, I would eventually have to speak to them, if only for a polite "Nice day, isn't it?" As a Southerner, being in close proximity with another human being for more than five minutes requires social graces to speak to those nearby and make small talk. I knew etiquette would not allow me to escape the sad situation without speaking to my neighbors, and I was right.

"H-ow are y-y-you?" The Broken Man let the words scrape past his throat and dribble out of his mouth as he craned his head to look at me past his wife.

I smiled with quiet empathy, sincerity, and a touch of pity. "I'm fine. How are you?"

He met my canned reply with, "I'm good-d. Cc-an you under-stand me?"

Well, crap. I thought I might get away with just the typical small talk, but he obviously wanted to talk, really talk, to me.

Without showing my frustration with the sudden awkward social situation, I told him I could indeed understand him. His wife never once looked up from her magazine, until he started telling me the following, at which point she stared intently at her husband: "Sometimes my wife gets confused, and she takes off all her clothes. If I fall asleep in this waiting room and she does that, please wake me up."

My heart pounded against my ribcage; my palms dampened my phone's protective case. I got light-headed at the perplexity of the situation. It was obvious that the Broken Man was very ill, and all his ailments must have affected his reasoning and logic; otherwise he wouldn't be telling me such a thing. What do I do? Oh, God, what do I say?!

I smiled politely, not at all sincerely, and told him I'd be sure to let him know if that happened. I thought it right to meet him on his level, share in his fantasy world, and let him think he was the healthier between he and his wife. This poor, poor man.

His wife slowly looked back at me with an expression I could not read. She then looked down at her magazine as she rolled it up and proceeded to hit her husband in the arm with it. They both burst out in laughter.

"Sorry," she said. "My husband has a horrible sense of humor." She settled back into her chair with a sigh of contentedness.

My head was reeling. I recovered long enough to mutter, "I have one of those too." I'm not even sure what that meant. They were just the only words that would come out.

She said, "What? A husband with a bad sense of humor?"

I laughed some more and nodded.

That was the end of our short conversation. They returned to their magazine and window-watching. I sat there trying not to look shocked. My little sphere of comfort had burst. It suddenly wasn't just me sitting in a waiting room chair; it was me, two administrative assistants, a couple of dozen patients, and just as many family members. I felt so exposed, as if I was the one who got confused and took off all my clothes.

Never in my life had I been so deftly removed from one opinion to the complete opposite, and never would I have thought that the Broken Man would be the one to do that to me. He seemed so incapable of, well, lots of things; how could he make me go from feeling pity for him to feeling pity and shame for myself in the span of a few sentences? He did all this while his wife sat beside him, expecting it. She had no doubt in him or his ability to change someone's life with a short conversation.

As I rolled the moment over and over again in my mind, the man was called back to see the doctor. The wife put down her magazine and took her place behind her husband's wheelchair like a useless sentry and began to push him toward the open door.

With one last bit of cognizance and humility, I told the man to keep an eye on his wife. They were already through the door. I'm not even sure he heard me. I wanted him to laugh, react to my pitiful attempt at a joke so that he knew that I knew that he'd changed me, the Broken Woman, for the better.

Willie Nelson Goes to Church

by Keith Hall

You have to take it on faith that my dog Hank is well trained. I mean, he's a field trial champion. But Willie Nelson—well, he's just a leggy, know-nothing, goofy puppy yet. So it was a Sunday morning last fall when I was outside with my fellas. Bad dog owner that I am, I had them off the leash. We live at Eighth and Commerce in downtown Little Rock, and there is a little strip of green grass, next lot over. They were sniffing and peeing and tussling and rolling around and just being dogs, you know? And this guy came walking down the street, across the street, carrying a transparent bag full of loaves and buns and scones and croissants and dinner rolls and maybe even an English muffin or two.

Once the bread man got past us, across the street mind you, Willie got interested in him and ran across the street after him. The man stopped and Willie was dancing around him, jumping up on him and sniffing the sack. I told Hank to sit where he was and I crossed the street, apologized to the bread man and got Willie Nelson by the collar and we went back to our grass lot where Hank was waiting for us. The bread man carried on.

The next corner, toward downtown, is Eighth and Rock. First Lutheran Church sits on that corner across Rock Street from me. As the bread man drew near the corner, Willie Nelson bolted again and ran the length of the block out in Eighth Street, angling across the pavement toward the bread guy, who was now rounding the corner onto Rock. This time he did not stop and Willie kept walking with him. Honestly, I really needed to put Hank in the back yard before I took off after Willie. But I needed to move quickly, so I told Hank to "sit" in my front yard. Hank knows what "sit" means. I mean, he's a solid sitter. The technical term for it is "steady." We have spent countless hours training which always includes some formal "sitting." So Hank "sat" and I took off after Willie and the bread man.

As I was jogging up Eighth on this nice October Sunday morning, I noticed the doors to the church were wide open, inviting. Not only the big heavy outside doors but the ones to the sanctuary, too. From outside, I could see the backs of the faithful, gathered there to worship. As I came to the corner, Hank bolted from my yard and ran the length of the block, out in the street, angling across, and joined me on the corner. I reared back and sternly boomed "SIT" as I whacked him hard, open handed, on his rear. I looked up and realized, to my great concern, Willie and the bread man were turning onto Seventh. I took about five steps when a red pick-up screeched to a halt at the corner where I had just left Hank, sitting pretty as a picture now, across from the church. The guy in the truck yelled threateningly, "Hey, buddy, hit that dog again."

I yelled back, "Excuse me?"

"Hit that dog again and you go to the hospital."

"Man, you don't have any idea what's going on here. This is a well trained dog, and he's my dog."

The guy yelled, "Well, it is my world and I don't want to see that kind of ugliness in it."

As I yelled my string of expletives back, I looked up to see them closing the sanctuary doors to the church. The guy in the truck peeled off and I resumed my chase of Willie and the bread man who were now out of sight up Seventh Street. And Hank just sat.

I raced to Seventh and when I turned the corner, to my relief I saw that Willie Nelson had gotten involved with some dogs on leashes being walked my way. The bread man was a speck on the horizon, now, way the heck up Seventh, and no longer of interest to any of us. The dog-walkers became hip to my chase of Willie and collared him and held him until I got there. I thanked them, gathered up Willie and headed back for Hank and then home. Traffic was coming, and we couldn't cross the street so we walked the block on the same side as the church but across from Hank. Some more cars were coming so I was eying Hank and praying that he did not dart out in front of them to cross to us. He did not.

When it was our turn to cross, I stepped into the crosswalk. And that's when I looked up to see Willie running up the stairs and in through the big outside doors of the church. I figured, okay, they closed the sanctuary doors; I'll just slip up in the foyer and get me my puppy. Oh, no. Not that easy. They had not closed the aisle doors, and to my horror, when I got to the foyer, I saw Willie Nelson prancing down the side aisle.

I have no idea whether the congregation was looking at Willie or giggling at me or what, because I only had eyes for Willie Nelson. I stood at the head of the aisle and in my loudest stage whisper called, "Willie. Willie. Willie Nelson." And about halfway down the aisle he stopped, and startled, looked around at those few good Christians scattered around that sacred sanctuarial space, and he spooked.

Maybe he'd heard me. Maybe he'd heard The Word. Maybe he heard The Word and spooked. Maybe he heard The Word and imagined himself lolling forever on some vibrant grassy strip with those faithful Lutherans, gorged fat on broken fishes and multiplied loaves; wasted, on once water wine. Maybe he heard The Word and he did not want to be washed in any blood from any lamb. Whatever.

Willie Nelson turned his back on the preacher, tucked his tail, and came slinking out to me in the foyer. I grabbed him by the collar, bounced down the outside stairs, and crossed the street. Hank was still sitting ever so faithfully, so I gave him the okay and released him.

He and Willie Nelson danced around each other and me as we all three headed home.

Hook, Line and Stinker

by Sandra Spotts-Hamilton

I'm not sure how it happened that the four of us ended up in a john boat that sticky, hot August day, but I suspect it began with a plan of Daddy's to spend the day in peace and solitude and to get his limit of bass and bream to boot. An announcement, "I'm goin' fishin'," was met with "not without us, you aren't," from Mama, and "please, please can we go?" from us two girls. And it probably sounded simple enough to Daddy: take Mama and the girls and at least come home with a few more bream. So we packed the car with the cane poles, Daddy's tackle box, rod and reel, worm bucket, cricket cage, thermos of ice water, and the old metal ice chest packed with pimento cheese sandwiches and Barq's "cold drinks," as we called them, even though they weren't cold yet. We stopped at a roadside bait shop and filled the bucket and the cage and bought ice to fill the chest. We rolled down the windows and settled into the thirty-minute road trip, which seemed like it covered a hundred miles.

Daddy rented the boat and motor as we hauled all of the gear out of the car and loaded it into the boat. He took his place by the outboard and the three of us precariously stepped aboard.

In those pre-sunscreen days, my parents' solution to preventing our Scots-Irish delicate skin from frying was to cover it. So in the fierce August blaze we sat in a boat with hats, long-sleeved flannel shirts, jeans, socks, and shoes. No, we wouldn't burn, but we were melting underneath the garb. We could have survived a nor'easter in that gear.

And so, Daddy fired up the motor, and we were launched into the trip that later would become family lore and a metaphor for how we operated as a family unit.

Lake Conway is a manmade lake, created by flooding acres of trees and brush, which made it a good fishing lake. At the same time, the submerged timber made for perilous boating. Every few yards, the motor would moan and Dad would cuss, rocking the boat to release it from the stump that it was lodged on, and we would scream in terror that we would capsize.

We finally made it to a brushy cove that Dad figured was a good area for us to bream fish while he cast for bass. As soon as he baited the three hooks and made his first cast, one of us, including Mama, would get our hooks tangled in the brush and whine "Daaadddeeee, help!" We would see his trademark scowl develop as he tucked his rod under his arm and leaned in to undo the mess and then reloaded the hook. He cautioned us to quiet our voices so that we did not frighten away the fish. I have a feeling it was also his intention to get himself some relief. The pattern continued to repeat itself, changing only with whose hook was caught on the brush, or who had their bait nibbled off by a small bream that knew better than to gulp down the whole meal at once.

One bass taunted Dad by taking the bait connected to the loosely held rod and taking off with it. He paddled furiously after it, leaning as far as he could without going in head-first to grab it, saying less and less as the outing dragged on under the relentless blazing sun. In spite of us, Daddy managed to pull in some nice bass, which he threaded on the stringer and hung in the water by his side of the boat to keep them alive. We even caught some good keeper bream, but that meant he had to stop to take them off the hook and reload the bait every time. Every now and then I would see him bring the stringer up, softening his scowl ever so slightly, as if to say, "At least, at the end of this ordeal, I will have some good fish to fry."

A few minutes of peace for Daddy would go by before the combination of boredom, Barq's cold drinks, and the sound of water lapping against the side of the boat had at least one of us whining, "I gotta go bathroom—now." So we all were ordered out onto the snaky bank to do our business, fast. We complied with the "fast" order in fear that he would leave us all there to become food for vermin lurking in the woods. But then, in another half hour, someone had to go again.

At last, Dad said, "Pull us out some of those sandwiches, Shorty. Let's have a little bite of lunch."

I reached in the old metal ice chest and found our four limp, soggy sandwiches floating outside of the built-in food tray like white slabs of driftwood. The wax paper wrappers and the tray had been no match for Daddy's jostling stump-release technique. My parents, having been raised during the depression, believed in no-frills food, so "we're having pimento cheese" meant just that and only that. I envied my friends who had fancy school lunches packed with multiple courses— sandwiches and chips and pickles and cupcakes wrapped in real sandwich wrap instead of used bread sacks. Daddy was the original Recycle Man before it was cool—way before. So on this day, too, there were no frills and no other food except for the can of vi-eenies Daddy found in this tackle box. He ran his rusty can opener around the edges, poured the juice and the indeterminable white gunk off the top and offered the can to us. We knew better than to refuse them, so each of us grabbed a sausage and made it last so we wouldn't be offered another.

The adventure continued on, with more tangling, whining, peeing, and cussing. Daddy was not one to pull out of a situation when the going got rough. As the relentless noon sun bore down on us, I began to feel very fuzzy and nauseous, and I noticed Sister was staring with dull eyes at her cork with no reaction to its bobbing.

The heat was taking its toll on us, and we must have been teetering on the edge of heat exhaustion, a condition that was foreign to my parents. I felt myself fading away from the lake, away from the boat, and away from my family, when a wave of Barq's Strawberry cold drink came up from my stomach into my mouth and into the boat.

How brilliant! Had I been able to do that voluntarily, ending this nightmare on the lake earlier, I would have.

With that act, Dad thrust his handkerchief at Sister, who was sharing the seat with me, saying, "Clean her up, Mo." Mama, who was in the front seat, jumped up with intentions of coming to my aid, but promptly slipped and sat down in the bottom of the boat, which by now was a reservoir holding a slurry of muddy lake water and regurgitated Barq's Strawberry cold drink. The lake echoed her yelling, "Bud! Bud!"

As if it were one motion, Daddy whipped in his line, tossed the rod in the boat, jerked the outboard on, and pulled up the one prize he was awarded for getting through this day, the stringer, and found himself clutching a bouquet of bass and bream heads and skeletons—the remains of the feast we had provided for the turtles of Lake Conway. He threw it in the boat, muttering, "Ain't that a bird dog." And with that, we cut through the murky water, banging against stumps, brush, floating logs, and other boats. Sister and I jumped onto the bank and, without being told, unloaded the boat and packed the car. We took off for home in total silence at last for Dad. Peace always comes with a price.

That was our one and only fishing excursion as a family. From that day forward, Daddy invited only one of us at a time to fish or hunt with him.

And that was just fine.

Contributors

Helen Austin, a resident of Little Rock for almost thirty years, has been a newspaper and magazine food writer and performing arts reviewer.

Tim Bennett has lived in the South for thirty-seven years. He is a high school Spanish teacher who also works with creative writing students. He has taught for twenty years, and he also has worked as a radio news director and announcer as well as a feature writer and news reporter. He and his wife Marla live in Batesville, Arkansas.

Arthur Paul Bowen is a lawyer and writer who lives in the People's Republic of Hillcrest here in Little Rock. He is a frequent contributor to this show. His writing has appeared in the *Dallas Morning News*, the *Arkansas Democrat-Gazette*, the *Arkansas Times* and *Soirée* Magazine.

Kevin Brockmeier has lived in Little Rock since he was four years old and considers himself a native of the city. He is the author of the novels *The Illumination*, *The Brief History of the Dead*, and *The Truth about Celia*; the children's novels *City of Names* and *Grooves: A Kind of Mystery*; and the story collections, *Things that Fall from the Sky* and *The View from the Seventh Layer*. His work has been translated into sixteen languages, and he has published his stories in such venues as *The New Yorker*, the *Georgia Review*, *McSweeney's*, *Zoetrope: All-Story*, *Tin House*, the *Oxford American*, *The Best American Short Stories*, *The Year's Best Fantasy and Horror*, and *New Stories from the South*. He has received the Borders Original Voices award, three O. Henry awards (one a first prize), the PEN USA award, a Guggenheim Fellowship, and an NEA grant. Recently he was named one of Grantham Magazine's Best Young American Novelists. Brockmeier is also the recipient of the 2011 William F. Laman Public Library Writer's Fellowship.

Velda Brotherton writes historical fiction and nonfiction, and she has twelve published books. For twenty years, her historical articles have appeared in several newspapers in Northwest Arkansas. She lives in Winslow, Arkansas with her husband Don.

Amy Manning Burns is a graduate student in the University of Arkansas at Little Rock's writing and rhetoric program. She lives in Little Rock with her husband Jay and their baby boy, Evan. Sections of this story appeared in UALR's journal of nonfiction, *Quills and Pixels*, in 2008.

C. Allan Butkus is the author of four published books: *The Thinking Rocks*, *The Vampire's Fourth Feather*, *The Vampire's Secret*, and *Upstairs with Angelina*. In the last five years, he has won twenty-eight awards for prose and poetry.

Marcia Camp has been a freelance writer for over thirty-five years. Her short stories, features, essays, and poetry have appeared in periodicals and literary journals locally and nationally. She was nominated for a Pushcart Prize 2004.

Mare Carmody is a voice actor, musician, and writer living in Asheville, North Carolina. She collects dogs and guitars.

Judith Waller Carroll lived in San Francisco and Montana before moving to a new life in the South. She won the 2010 Carducci Poetry Prize from Tallahassee Writer's Association and lives in Hot Springs Village, Arkansas.

Hope Coulter is a novelist and poet who grew up in Alexandria, Louisiana, an excruciating seventy miles from "The Lake." She lives in Little Rock and teaches creative writing at Hendrix College.

Jacob Craig grew up in Hot Springs, Arkansas and currently lives in Little Rock. He is chattier with his family and a little more honest with the clergy now. He is working on a memoir.

Jill Duvall is a clinical social worker who lives in Hot Springs, Arkansas and works in Little Rock. Her crazy mother was a writer, and Jill is hoping to finish her book *Musing of a Manic Depressive* someday.

Susan Elder is a North Little Rock native and is the director of the Jim Elder Good Sport Fund. She is proud to say this is her fourth story on *Tales from the South*. After thirty years in Dallas and New York, she returned to Little Rock five years ago, and she knows she is exactly where she is supposed to be.

Jay Freidrich was born and raised in Little Rock. In his forty-year civil engineering career, he worked for the Army Corps of Engineers in Little Rock; Davis, California; and Washington D.C. He was a professor, department chair, and associate dean in the school for science and engineering for the University of Southern Indiana for twenty-four years. He returned home eight years ago, retiring as a professor emeritus. He and his wife Cecelia have three children and four grandchildren.

Hank Godwin is a long time resident of North Little Rock, and married to Liza, his wife of thirty-four years. He is worried, and hopeful, that his two wonderful sons will one day share similar embarrassing family experiences in public.

Graham Gordy completed his MFA in dramatic writing at NYU, where he received the Goldberg Award for Playwriting. His plays have been produced and performed by Naked Angels, the New Group, New York Stage and Film, the Drama Department, and the Royal Court of London. His work has been published in the *Oxford American*, *Imbibe* Magazine, *Arkansas Life*, and he writes a bi-weekly column for the *Arkansas Times*. Graham wrote the screenplay for *War Eagle, Arkansas*, and his TV pilot *The Wreck* was recently purchased by AMC. Graham was in New York for eight years until he missed home too much and came back. He still travels to L.A. every few months to peddle his wares, as he gets ninety-five percent of his work from out there.

Keith Hall practices law in Little Rock where he lives downtown with his lovely wife, and the apple of his eye, Freddy, who's never been to church, but is a fine retriever just the same.

Lawrence Hamilton received a bachelor's degree in music education from Henderson State University in Arkadelphia, Arkansas, and has performed as a dancer with BalleTap USA, The Brooklyn Dance Theatre, and Southern Ballet Theatre. He has worked as a vocal coach and arranger with many artists in the recording industry including Marky Mark and the Funky Bunch (Mark Walhberg), the New Kids on the Block, Jordan Knight, and Joe McIntyre. Lawrence has served as musical director for opera diva Jessye Norman in "Jessye Norman Sings for the Healing of AIDS," which included performances by Elton John, Whoopi Goldberg, Toni Morrison, Max Roach, Bill T. Jones, Anna De Vere Smith, and a sixty-voice choir. He has performed in concert with the legendary Lena Horne, for President and Mrs. Ronald Reagan at the White House, for Ambassador and Mrs. Thomas Pickering at the U.S. embassy in Moscow, and Pope John Paul II at the Vatican. He has been inducted into the Arkansas Entertainer's Hall of Fame and the Arkansas Black Hall of Fame. And he's got a street named after him in his hometown. He is currently working on his memoir entitled, *In an Ordinary Life*, from which his story is adapted.

Jeremy Harper is an advertising writer living in the city of Little Rock. He arrived in the South at the age of six and has been working to improve his Southern drawl ever since.

J.B. Hogan is an award-winning fiction writer, poet, local historian, and stand-up base player in a family band. His story "Kerosene Heat" was nominated for a 2010 Pushcart Prize. He lives in Fayetteville, Arkansas

Jay Jennings is a freelance writer whose journalism, book reviews, and humor have appeared in national magazines and newspapers, including *The New York Times*, *The Wall Street Journal*, *The Los Angeles Times*, the *Oxford American*, and *Travel and Leisure*. He is a regular contributor to *The New York Times* book review. He began his writing career as a reporter at *Sports Illustrated*, where he covered college football and basketball, followed by four years as editor at *Tennis Magazine*. While at the latter, he edited an anthology of short stories and poetry: *Tennis and the Meaning of Life: A Literary Anthology of the Game*, which *The New Yorker* called, "a delight and perhaps a surprise to those who know and care about literature." His work has been recognized by *The Best American Sports Writing* annual and has appeared in the humor anthology *Mirth of a Nation: Best Contemporary Humor*. He is a two time MacDowell Colony fellow of fiction and was awarded in 2008 from the Arkansas Arts Council for a novel in progress. His critically acclaimed 2010 book, *Race, Football, and the Soul of the American City*, chronicles one season of Little Rock Central High School's football team and the community around it, fifty years after the school's tumultuous integration of the Little Rock Nine.

J.H.E. "Excy" Johnston was born in Baltimore, Maryland and raised in the southwest. As an architect, Excy worked throughout the country, and even in London, England, but he and his wife Amy call central Arkansas home.

Kandy Jones is an artist, speaker, teacher, writer, and junk specialist. Most folks know her as the garage sale queen from her many appearances on KATV Channel 7 *Daybreak*. She is one of the original founders of the Argenta Revitalization Movement and still lives in the Argenta Historic District of North Rock, Arkansas with her husband Jimmy Brewy.

Sharolyn Jones-Taylor is a middle-age Southern woman working to convince herself that the serenity she hears comes with age is much more satisfying than the firmness that comes with youth. Thus far, she remains unconvinced.

Daniel Koehler has published four novels and numerous short stories available electronically from the Amazon Kindle Store, Apple iBooks, and Nook Books. He lives in Little Rock with his wife Edna and three children.

Mara Leveritt is a veteran Arkansas reporter, editor at *Arkansas Times*, and the author of two nonfiction books about crime and public corruption. In her capacities as journalist and activist, she has been named Arkansas Journalist of the Year for her investigative reporting and Arkansas Abolitionist of the Year for her work to end the death penalty. Leveritt is the author of *Boys on the Track* and *Devil's Knot*, published in 2002 about the deeply problematic trials about the men known as the West Memphis Three. Leveritt continues to write about that case for the *Arkansas Times* and online media, and she was a leader in the movement seeking new trials for the men, who were freed in 2011. Leveritt has two children and five grandchildren. She was born in Chicago, grew up in Denver, and moved to Arkansas at twenty-three. She hopes to be buried in Little Rock's Mount Holly Cemetery.

Rod Lorenzen manages the book publishing division for the Butler Center for Arkansas Studies at the Central Arkansas Library System. A former long-time bookseller in Little Rock, he also is a co-editor of the book *Homecoming: The Southern Family in Short Fiction.*

Buck Marsh was born in May 16, 1923 in Florence, Alabama. He's been married for sixty-two years and has three children, seven grandchildren, and one great-grandchild. Though wounded in battle, Buck is a survivor of World War II as an infantry soldier in Belgium and Germany, where he earned three battle stars and the Purple Heart. He is retired from the construction industry, and he and his wife Wanda make their home in Alabama.

Nathan McKinney loves his wife Susie and children Ginger and Baker. He loves working for the University of Arkansas Division of Agriculture. He loves to fish. But he REALLY loves his dogs, Toby and BrightEyes.

Betty McPherson wrote and directed her first play in 1996 with four more original productions following. She has held the position of Office Manager at SCM Architects for the past eighteen years, and she enjoys tooting around with the top down in her Mazda Miata with her four-legged son, Jake.

Evelyn Menz is a Pine Bluff, Arkansas native, a graduate of the University of Arkansas at Fayetteville, and after twenty-eight years of teaching, is retired and a volunteer. She likes to travel with her wonderful husband David, read, and play tennis all with her old and newly placed parts. She is a twelve-year breast cancer survivor.

Dottie Lou Norwood has a Bachelor of Arts with majors in English and history, and a Masters in Administrative Education with Superintendency certification. She has worked as an Educational Consultant and a part-time professor at the University of Arkansas in Little Rock. She is an aspiring author.

Jennifer Pierce-Mathus is an accomplished Southern actor and writer, working in sketch comedy and appearing in numerous TV and film roles, including the award-winning short "Antiquities" and the Hank Williams bio-pic, *The Last Ride*. A freelancer by day, she has completed her first screenplay and lives in Oxford, Mississippi, with her husband, musician Jimbo Mathus, and French bulldog, Lola Jolene.

Laura Rakes, M.A., is a grant writer and editor for the UAMS Center for Distance Health and ANGELS Program. Past appointments include Managing Editor for *Literature and Medicine*, a Johns Hopkins's publication, multiple freelance writing and editing opportunities, and instructor of Composition II at UALR. Despite all this, she still really enjoys writing for fun and does so whenever she is not busy spending time with her son, Dexter, husband, Sam, and their three dogs.

Megan Riley is in the graduate writing program at the University of New Orleans. She composes art with black pens and white keys.

Rex Robbins and his wife Sandy live in North Little Rock. He is an environmental engineer by trade and training, but enjoys writing and is currently gathering stories from the Buffalo River Valley.

Bradi Roberts hails from Bald Knob, Arkansas. She has more degrees than a pot of boiling water, and previously worked in education, ministry, journalism, and hospitality management. Today she works as a freelance editor for clients in Melbourne, San Francisco, Baltimore, Austin, and Portland, which means she stays in her pajamas and lives inside the internet.

Joy Rockenbach was born in the heat of the Mississippi Delta and knows a good funeral from a bad one. Her many friends have always encouraged her to write some of her Delta stories. Some of these friends have helped Joy plan her own audacious funeral complete with multiple dress and hat changes. Should only last about two days.

Joanna J. Seibert has been an ordained deacon in the Episcopal Church for ten years, and is a pediatric radiologist at Arkansas Children's Hospital. She has lived in Little Rock since 1976 with her husband Robert, three children, and now six grandchildren, but she travels to the Gulf Coast at least four times a year to renew her spirit.

Lynn Schaefer spent the first eighteen years of her life in Nashville, Arkansas and returned to her home state in 1991 after living in Dallas, West Africa, and Boston. She teaches English as a second language at University of Central Arkansas in Conway.

Darinda Sharp was born and raised in Fayetteville, Arkansas by Carolyn and Roy Sharp. She now lives in Little Rock. Darinda is writing her first novel.

Jack Shock has the world's best job at Harding University where he teaches for free, but they have to pay him to grade papers. When he's not traveling, he's sitting on his back porch with his dog Helen thinking about traveling.

Sandra Spotts-Hamilton is from Little Rock and describes herself as a late-blooming baby boomer who dances to the strum of a different guitar. She believes it's never too late to follow your dreams or to seek divinity.

Grif Stockley is an award-winning author, groundbreaking historian, playwright, and former legal aid attorney who is committed on all fronts to shining a light on racial injustice and upholding individual civil rights. At the completion of his tour of duty, Grif received his Juris Doctorate degree from the University of Arkansas at Fayetteville, and launched a thirty-one-year career with the Center for Arkansas Legal Services, representing indigent and working class people in civil law cases. Grif has six published novels, five of which were published by Simon and Schuster and feature his memorable lawyer protagonist, Gideon Page. His nonfiction works began with *Blood in their Eyes: The Elaine Race Massacres of 1919*, which jumpstarted his contributions as a historian of race relations. This book was followed by three more ground-breaking nonfiction books centered around race relations in the South. Grif has won numerous literary and historical awards. Twice he won the John Ragsdale award for the best book on Arkansas History, the first for his biography of Daisy Bates, and most recently *Ruled by Race: Black/White Relations in Arkansas, from Slavery to the Present*. He was inducted into the Arkansas Writers Hall of Fame in 2001, and he was the first Dee Brown Fellow at the Butler Center for Arkansas studies. In March 2010 Grif became the first recipient of an annual $10,000 grant bestowed by the William F. Laman Public Library Writers Foundation. His latest book is about the 1959 fire at the former Negro Boys Industrial School in Wrightsville, Arkansas that killed twenty-one teenagers locked inside a dormitory.

Krystal Suit was born in Colorado, to a family with more history than she knew. The climax of their story takes place in Georgia, the falling action in Arkansas. A recent graduate of Hendrix College, Krystal sets out now with an English degree in hand, searching for the next beginning.

Phillip Taylor is an instructor in the intensive English program at the University of Central Arkansas. He is a freelance writer, author, and musician from Malvern, Arkansas and currently resides with his fiancé Leanne in Searcy, Arkansas. Phillip wrote as a guest columnist for several editions of *Nsync* magazine from 2008 to 2010 and has recently finished his first novel. He is also working on a collection of creative nonfiction short stories and essays to be published in the near future.

Frank Thurmond lives in his hometown of Little Rock, Arkansas where he teaches literature in the English department of the University of Arkansas at Little Rock. His work has appeared in various publications including *The International Herald Tribune* and the *Arkansas Democrat Gazette*. In addition to writing his new memoir, Thurmond is a screenwriter and is currently working on producing a slate of feature films through his L.A. based production company.

Susan Toone lives Little Rock with her husband and two daughters. She writes a blog called *Rants from an Old Trout*, and to make money, she works as a technical writer and trainer. Thanks to being part of this project, she feels like a celebrity.

Margie Tubbs is a native of Shreveport, Louisiana. She has worked as a journalist, a deputy sheriff, and a special education teacher. She resides in Mobile, Alabama with her husband Dennis. She is retired and is writing whenever the mood hits.

John Wells is from Little Rock. He writes a weekly newsletter for craft beer enthusiasts, dedicated to providing craft beer news, education and information on upcoming events. His email is John@JohnTheBeerSnob.com, and his website is JohnTheBeerSnob.Com.

Stan Whisman escaped from Oklahoma ten years ago and now lives in the mountains near Mountainview, Arkansas with the love of his life wife. He poses as a mild-mannered retirement community manager by day and plays banjo by night.

Madelyn F. Young, a retired teacher and school administrator, has always loved children. She lives in Hot Springs, Arkansas where she is active in the Village Writers' Club. Madelyn has won numerous awards for her stories, memoirs, and essays.

Acknowledgments

First, thanks to Jeff Baskin at William F. Laman Public Library for believing in me and Tales. Laman provided the seed money to take us to the next level, and sponsors each of our Tin Roof Projects. I am forever grateful for your vision, Jeff, and your confidence in me. Also, thank you to John and Donna and the Argenta Arts Foundation. And to Vicky and Angela at *AY Magazine* for believing in us and adding our stories to the magazine.

Many thanks to Stephanie for your tireless work in helping us stay organized, and to Kandy for your insight in the early stages. Debra, you keep me on my toes and in the know, and your ideas for the show are creative and smart. I appreciate you more than you know.

Thanks, Jay, for making me and the show sound so good, and for being willing to let me bounce my (sometimes crazy) ideas off of you. Thank you, Mark, for the great theme music and for showing up to play each and every show. You rock. And to all the musicians, especially The Salty Dogs and Bonnie Montgomery: thanks for making the show come alive.

Many, many thanks to KUAR for our 6th Season, and to Chef Jason and all of the staff at Starving Artist Café for banging out more than 100 dinners in an hour and a half every Tuesday night. We're all in awe.

More than anything, I want to thank all of the hundred and sixty writers from Season 6 for your bravery. Sharing your stories has bridged generations, regions, races, and even countries. And we are all better for it.

Grateful acknowledgment to the following publications where stories or earlier versions of stories first appeared:

"Missing Pages" by Amy Manning Burns. Excerpted from "A Short History of Men," *Quills and Pixels*, September 2011.

"Ozark Beats" by J.B. Hogan. *Dead Mule*, January 2009.

"Seasons" by Kevin Brockmeier. Previously published as three separate stories: "July, Little Rock, 1983," *Arkansas Life*, July 2010. "Three and a Half Snows," *Spirit Magazine*, November 2007. "Last Words," *The New York Times Magazine*, July 27, 2008.

"The Last Days of Ray Winder Field" by Jay Jennings. *Elysian Fields Quarterly*, Vol. 26, No. 2: 2007.

"The Nesting Loon" by Susan Toone. Previously published as "The Waiting Game," *Adoption Today*, Aug/Sept 2006.